FUNDAMENTALS
of the Faith

JAMES C. MORRIS

Fundamentals of the Faith
Copyright © 2023 by James C. Morris

the author may be contacted at:
20 Spring Drive Place
Ocala, FL 34472-3008

author's e-mail address:
james-morris@sbcglobal.net

All rights reserved. No part of this publication may be reproduced, stored in a retrieval system, or transmitted in any way by any means, electronic, mechanical, photocopy, recording, or otherwise, without the prior permission of the copyright owner, except as provided by USA copyright law.

Scripture taken from the New King James Version.
Copyright © 1979, 1980, 1982 by Thomas Nelson, Inc.
Used by permission. All rights reserved.

Bible text from the New King James Version is not to be reproduced in copies or otherwise by any means except as permitted in writing by Thomas Nelson, Inc., Attn: Bible Rights and Permissions, P.O. Box 141000, Nashville, TN 37214-1000.

Table of Contents

5 Introduction

7 **CHAPTER 1**
What Is Our Final Authority?

11 **CHAPTER 2**
The Sanctity of the Word of God

15 **CHAPTER 3**
Why Should We Believe In God?

21 **CHAPTER 4**
The Faithfulness of God

27 **CHAPTER 5**
The Love of God

31 **CHAPTER 6**
The Justice of God

35 **CHAPTER 7**
Who is Jesus?

45 **CHAPTER 8**
The Trinity

49 **CHAPTER 9**
Heaven

Page	Chapter	Title
57	CHAPTER 10	Hell
65	CHAPTER 11	Our Guilt Before God
71	CHAPTER 12	The Need for Repentance
75	CHAPTER 13	God's Provision for Our Guilt
81	CHAPTER 14	The Need to be Born Again
87	CHAPTER 15	The Need for Good Works
91	CHAPTER 16	Eternal Security
101	CHAPTER 17	But What About Sin In Our Lives?
109	CHAPTER 18	The Danger of Falling Away
115	CHAPTER 19	The Coming of Christ for His Own
121	CHAPTER 20	The Coming of Christ to Judge the Wicked
127	CHAPTER 21	The Coming of Christ to Deliver Israel
145		Conclusion

Introduction

In the last 50 or so years many churches have reached out to the communities around them, sometimes in earnest evangelism, and at other times more in the form of social relief. But one way or another, there has been a significant amount of outreach. This outreach has often been good, significant, and effective. But sadly, one critical element has often been neglected. This element, which is indeed critical, has been discipleship. The church has been fairly earnest in obeying our Lord's command to **"Go into all the world and preach the gospel to every creature."** (Mark 16:15) But it has been woefully inadequate in obeying the alternate statement of the great commission we find at the end of Matthew:

> **"Go therefore and make disciples of all the nations, baptizing them in the name of the Father and of the Son and of the Holy Spirit, teaching them to observe all things that I have commanded you; and lo, I am with you always,** *even* **to the end of the age."** (Matthew 28:19-20)

As the writer of these pages has traveled around among various churches, he has been distressed to observe a woeful degree of ignorance of the basic doctrines of the Christian faith. And here he is not speaking of any denomination in particular, but of the church in general. And even as these pages were being prepared, several pastors from different places have commented to him about how widespread this problem is. But he was also told that writing this would be a waste of time, "because no one reads anymore."

If it is indeed true that the general population has been so "dumbed down" that "no one reads anymore," it may seem like all is lost. But that is not the case.

For in spite of the fact that many people are unwilling to actually sit down and read such a publication as this, a faithful minister of the gospel can still use these pages as an outline to prepare a series of messages to build up the saints on the basic fundamentals of the Christian faith.

And by this is not meant the doctrines of any particular church or denomination, but the basic, fundamental teaching that is found in the Holy Scriptures. And as this writer has traveled around among many churches of many different denominations, he has witnessed a remarkable uniformity of doctrine among those that reverence the Word of God, the Bible, as it has come down to us.

So with these thoughts in mind, the following pages are sent out with the prayer that they might be used of God to build up the saints on their most holy faith.

> "But you, beloved, building yourselves up on your most holy faith, praying in the Holy Spirit, keep yourselves in the love of God, looking for the mercy of our Lord Jesus Christ unto eternal life." (Jude 1:20-21)

CHAPTER 1

What Is Our Final Authority?

What question could be more basic to any thinking process than, what is our thinking based upon? That is, what is the final authority that forms the basic foundation for our thinking?

Some people think this final authority should be our own minds. They want to define "truth" as whatever they think is true. Other people claim it should be the opinions of great minds. By this, they sometimes mean the opinions of people that were great in past ages, and sometimes mean the opinions of great leaders of the present time. Still others think it should be whatever most of the people in their particular society think. And others think it should be books like the Koran or the Vedas. But for a Christian, there is a different final authority. And that is whatever our God has told us in the Bible.

Now it is well and good to say this. But how do we know it is true? We need to see what the Bible says about itself. The most significant and absolute of these is in the recorded words of our Lord Jesus himself, when He said:

> "Do not think that I came to destroy the Law or the Prophets. I did not come to destroy but to fulfill. For assuredly, I say to you, till heaven and earth pass away, one jot or one tittle will by no means pass from the law till all is fulfilled." (Matthew 5:17-18)

To understand this, we need to know what the jot and the tittle were. These were the two smallest marks used in Hebrew writing.

From this, we understand that our Lord was saying that even the tiniest detail of everything written in the Bible was both absolutely accurate and important.

Again Jesus said:

> **"Do not think that I shall accuse you to the Father; there is *one* who accuses you – Moses, in whom you trust. For if you believed Moses, you would believe Me; for he wrote about Me. But if you do not believe his writings, how will you believe My words?"** (John 5:45-47)

Here, our Lord made it very plain that a belief of what Moses said was critical to believing in himself.

This last passage is particularly important in our day, because many people want to say they are Christians, but reject the creation account in the beginning of Genesis. But that account is both a part of **"the law,"** as Jesus referred to it, and is in one of the five books written by Moses. So both of these statements made by our Lord himself, make it very clear that an absolute belief in these things is a critical part of actually being a Christian, as opposed to just calling yourself a Christian.

Again, Jesus said **"It is written, That man shall not live by bread alone, but by every word of God."** (Luke 4:4) So Jesus clearly stressed the written Bible as both absolutely accurate in all of its tiniest details, and critically import to both our beliefs and our lives.

But there is more. For the Apostle Peter wrote that:

> **"no prophecy of Scripture is of any private interpretation, for prophecy never came by the will of man, but holy men of God spoke *as they were* moved by the Holy Spirit."** (2 Peter 1:20-21)

Peter also wrote:

> "our beloved brother Paul, according to the wisdom given to him, has written to you, as also in all his epistles, speaking in them of these things, in which are some things hard to understand, which untaught and unstable *people* twist to their own destruction, as *they do* also the rest of the Scriptures." (2 Peter 3:15-16)

So now, in addition to the words of our Lord himself, we have the words of the one Apostle that many consider the most authoritative of them all, clearly stating of all **"Scripture,"** that it **"never came by the will of man, but holy men of God spoke *as they were moved by the Holy Spirit,*"** and that the writings of Paul were also "Scriptures," like those of the Old Testament.

In this short summary, I have only covered the high points of what the Bible says about itself. But a computer search of the entire Bible showed the following wording to be found in the Bible, as rendered in the NKJV version:

> **"Thus says the Lord"** is found 420 times.
> **"The word of the Lord"** is found 262 times. And four of these times add the word "God" to the end, making it **"The word of the Lord God."**
> **"The Lord spoke"** is found 138 times.
> **"The word of God"** is found 45 times.
> **"The words of the Lord"** is found 19 times.
> **"God spoke"** is found 12 times.
> **"The Lord says"** is found 10 times.
> **"The Spirit says"** is found 7 times.
> **"The words of God"** is found 6 times.
> **"God says"** is found 6 times.
> **"The Spirit said"** is found twice.

And finally, **"Says the Spirit," "The word of the Holy One,"** and **"The words of the Holy One"** are each found once.

So in conclusion, we need to remember the exhortation Paul gave Timothy.

> "But you must continue in the things which you have learned and been assured of, knowing from whom you have learned *them*, and that from childhood you have known the Holy Scriptures, which are able to make you wise for salvation through faith which is in Christ Jesus."
> (2 Timothy 3:14-15)

This is what the Bible says about itself. Now this is either true, or it is not true. There can be no middle ground. Thus, if the Bible is not actually the word of God, as it clearly claims to be, then it is a fraud. And a fraud is not a product of good men. It is inherently evil. So if the Bible is good, then it is, of necessity, what it claims to be, the very words of God himself. And if it is the very words of God, then it should indeed be accepted as the final authority for all of our thinking.

CHAPTER 2

The Sanctity of the Word of God

Throughout history, there have been people who have not liked what God said. So they pretended that He actually said something different. And some even dare to do this in our present time. But our God has warned them against this from one end of the Bible to the other. The first five books of the Bible were given through Moses, and in them we read:

> **"Whatever I command you, be careful to observe it; you shall not add to it nor take away from it."** (Deuteronomy 12:32)

And the Revelation, the last book in the Bible, is also the last book of the Bible to have been written. And at its end, we find these solemn words:

> **"For I testify to everyone who hears the words of the prophecy of this book: If anyone adds to these things, God will add to him the plagues that are written in this book; and if anyone takes away from the words of the book of this prophecy, God shall take away his part from the Book of Life, from the holy city, and *from* the things which are written in this book."** (Revelation 22:18-19)

And near the middle of the Bible we read:

> **"Do not add to His words, Lest He rebuke you, and you be found a liar."** (Proverbs 30:6)

So we are solemnly warned to not add anything to what the Bible says or take anything away from it. And why? Because:

> **"All Scripture *is* given by inspiration of God, and *is* profitable for doctrine, for reproof, for correction, for instruction in righteousness, that the man of God may be complete, thoroughly equipped for every good work."** (2 Timothy 3:16-17)

And, as we noticed in the last chapter, Jesus said:

> **"assuredly, I say to you, till heaven and earth pass away, one jot or one tittle will by no means pass from the law till all is fulfilled."** (Matthew 5:18)

As we also noted there, the jot and the tittle were the two smallest marks used in Hebrew writing, So our Lord was here saying that everything in the Bible is important, down to the tiniest detail. This means that we must not change anything at all in the entire Bible, no matter how tiny or insignificant we might think it is.

But there is another way to desecrate the very words of God. And that is to use God's exact words, but to use them in a deceptive manner. God calls this practice shameful, saying through the Apostle Paul:

> **"we have renounced the hidden things of shame, not walking in craftiness nor handling the word of God deceitfully."** (2 Corinthians 4:2)

And why is this so important? Because:

> **"Every word of God *is* pure; He *is* a shield to those who put their trust in Him."** (Proverbs 30:5)

And when Satan came to tempt our Lord, Jesus answered him by quoting Deuteronomy 8:3, saying:

> **"It is written, 'Man shall not live by bread alone, but by every word that proceeds from the mouth of God.'"** (Matthew 4:4 and Luke 4:4)

CHAPTER 3
Why Should We Believe In God?

We could come up with many logical reasons to try to convince people to believe in God. But the purpose of this book is not to come up with answers from our own reasoning, but to learn what God says about, well... everything. Our answers, my answers, may indeed be correct, or they may not be correct. But what God says is always correct. So our job is not to apply the reasonings of mere mortals to any other spiritual question, but to see what God says about it.

So what proof does God cite for His existence? First, we read in the New Testament that:

> **"since the creation of the world His invisible *attributes* are clearly seen, being understood by the things that are made, *even* His eternal power and Godhead, so that they are without excuse."** (Romans 1:20)

In this passage, God clearly says that unbelievers **"are without excuse,"** because **"His invisible *attributes* are clearly seen, being understood by the things that are made."** That is, that creation itself is the proof that God exists. And He says that this proof is so overwhelming that it leaves mankind **"without excuse."**

Again, we read that God:

> "did not leave Himself without witness, in that He did good, gave us rain from heaven and fruitful seasons, filling our hearts with food and gladness." (Acts 14:17) So God also says that His provision for our needs is also a witness to Himself.

But the great scripture, in which God first declared the witness of creation, is:

"The heavens declare the glory of God;

> And the firmament shows His handiwork.
> Day unto day utters speech,
> And night unto night reveals knowledge.
> There is no speech nor language
> *Where* their voice is not heard.
> Their line has gone out through all the earth,
> And their words to the end of the world.
> In them He has set a tabernacle for the sun,
> Which *is* like a bridegroom coming out of his chamber,
> *And* rejoices like a strong man to run its race.
> Its rising *is* from one end of heaven,
> And its circuit to the other end;
> And there is nothing hidden from its heat."
> (Psalm 19:1-6)

God himself considered this testimony so important that He quoted it in the book of Romans, saying:

> "But I say, have they not heard? Yes indeed: *'Their sound has gone out to all the earth, And their words to the ends of the world.'* " (Romans 10:18)

But why would God, who obviously has the power to prove anything, and to prove it in a way that cannot be denied, basically say, "This is the proof I offer, it is sufficient. And that is all the proof you are going to get"? The Holy Spirit answers this question by saying:

> **"For it is written: *'I will destroy the wisdom of the wise, And bring to nothing the understanding of the prudent.'* Where is the wise? Where is the scribe? Where is the disputer of this age? Has not God made foolish the wisdom of this world? For since, in the wisdom of God, the world through wisdom did not know God, it pleased God through the foolishness of the message preached to save those who believe. For Jews request a sign, and Greeks seek after wisdom; but we preach Christ crucified, to the Jews a stumbling block and to the Greeks foolishness, but to those who are called, both Jews and Greeks, Christ the power of God and the wisdom of God. Because the foolishness of God is wiser than men, and the weakness of God is stronger than men. For you see your calling, brethren, that not many wise according to the flesh, not many mighty, not many noble, *are called*. But God has chosen the foolish things of the world to put to shame the wise, and God has chosen the weak things of the world to put to shame the things which are mighty; and the base things of the world and the things which are despised God has chosen, and the things which are not, to bring to nothing the things that are, that no flesh should glory in His presence."** (1 Corinthians 1:19-29)

This last phrase is the key to the question we are examining. **"That no flesh should glory in His presence."** To God, "the nations *are* as a drop in a bucket, And are counted as the small dust on the scales." (Isaiah 40:15) How much less the intellect of a mere human. To Him, all such glorying by mere mortals, is simply nauseous.

But some might argue, with apparent logic, "Why would God cite such weak evidence for His existence, when we have so many available arguments that seem to us to us to be so very much stronger?" So the first question I will ask is, "How many of your arguments would be understood by a native in the Amazon jungle, who has never even learned to read, much less to understand the principles of modern science?" And after that, I will ask, "How many of the facts that have been actually proved by modern science, nullify or set aside these simple, and yet very logical, arguments?" And the answer to both of these questions is zero. For modern science claims it has proved many things. But when these claims are carefully examined, we learn that many of the "facts" that they so confidently throw around are not facts at all, but only theories.

And a simple persuasion about the existence of God is not enough. Indeed, God himself says:

> **"You believe that there is one God. You do well. Even the demons believe--and tremble!"** (James 2:19)

Simple acceptance in our minds that certain facts are correct is useless, unless that acceptance produces faith in our hearts.

> **"But without faith *it is* impossible to please *Him*, for he who comes to God must believe that He is, and *that* He is a rewarder of those who diligently seek Him."** (Hebrews 11:6)

This scripture says we need more than to just believe that "there is a God." We must not only believe **"that He is,"** but also that **"He is a rewarder of those who diligently seek Him."**

God has told us these things in his word, and He expects us to believe Him. Indeed when pressed for more proof, God's answer, through the mouth of his servant Abraham, was:

> **"They have Moses and the prophets; let them hear them."** (Luke 16:29) And **"If they do not hear Moses and the prophets, neither will they be persuaded though one rise from the dead."** (Luke 16:31)

So the real question is, do you choose to believe what God has told us? The eternal destiny of your soul hangs on your answer to this one simple question.

CHAPTER 4

The Faithfulness of God

Aside from the very existence of God, and the identity of Jesus, there could hardly be a single doctrine more fundamental to the Christian faith than the faithfulness of God. For without that, we have zero basis for our faith. Although our God has made many promises to them that love Him, how do we know that He will keep those promises? It is because of His faithfulness, the absolute reliability of every promise he has ever made, to us or to anyone else. If God is not absolutely faithful, we have zero basis for our faith. This is our only hope, the only basis for our trust in Him. This is not just some idea invented by Christian teachers, but our God himself appeals to His faithfulness as the reason we should trust Him. For we read:

> **"Let us hold fast the confession of *our* hope without wavering, for He who promised is faithful."** (Hebrews 10:23) And again, **"He who calls you *is* faithful, who also will do *it*."** (1 Thessalonians 5:24)

And even the first time our God mentioned this subject, He said:

> **"Therefore know that the LORD your God, He is God, the faithful God who keeps covenant and mercy for a thousand generations with those who love Him and keep His commandments."** (Deuteronomy 7:9)

The Holy Spirit also insists upon the faithfulness of our Lord Jesus, saying in Revelation 1:5, **"Jesus Christ, the faithful witness,"** and by calling Him **"the Amen, the Faithful and True Witness, the Beginning of the creation of God"** in Revelation 3:14, and by saying:

> **"Therefore, holy brethren, partakers of the heavenly calling, consider the Apostle and High Priest of our confession, Christ Jesus, who was faithful to Him who appointed Him, as Moses also was *faithful* in all His house."** (Hebrews 3:1-2)

Our God not only insists upon His own faithfulness, but on the faithfulness of His word. Jesus said:

> **"Do not think that I came to destroy the Law or the Prophets. I did not come to destroy but to fulfill. For assuredly, I say to you, till heaven and earth pass away, one jot or one tittle will by no means pass from the law till all is fulfilled."** (Matthew 5:17-18)

And 2 Peter 1:19 Says of **"the prophetic word"** that:

> **"you do well to heed as a light that shines in a dark place, until the day dawns and the morning star rises in your hearts."**

So we read that **"All Your commandments *are* faithful."** (Psalm 119:86) And **"Your testimonies, *which* You have commanded, *Are* righteous and very faithful."** (Psalm 119:138) And again, at the end of the Bible, we read that **"these words are true and faithful"** in Revelation 21:5, and **"These words are faithful and true."** In Revelation 22:6. And one of the qualifications for a bishop, that is, a leader of a church, is that he must be **"holding fast the faithful word as he has been taught, that he may be able, by sound doctrine, both to exhort and convict those who contradict."** (Titus 1:9)

But our God not only declares His faithfulness. He also makes it exceedingly plain that He values our reliance upon that faithfulness. The first time we are told of this is in a story about Abraham, where we read:

> "Then Abram said, 'Look, You have given me no offspring; indeed one born in my house is my heir!' And behold, the word of the LORD *came* to him, saying, 'This one shall not be your heir, but one who will come from your own body shall be your heir.' Then He brought him outside and said, 'Look now toward heaven, and count the stars if you are able to number them.' And He said to him, 'So shall your descendants be.' And he believed in the LORD, and He accounted it to him for righteousness." (Genesis 15:3-6)

And in the New Testament, we are told of how God honored Sarah, Abraham's wife, for simply believing this promise. For we read:

> "By faith Sarah herself also received strength to conceive seed, and she bore a child when she was past the age, because she judged Him faithful who had promised. Therefore from one man, and him as good as dead, were born *as many* as the stars of the sky in multitude--innumerable as the sand which is by the seashore." (Hebrews 11:11-12)

But the New Testament also tells us why God recorded this actual historical event. For we are told that Abraham **"did not waver at the promise of God through unbelief, but was strengthened in faith, giving glory to God, and being fully convinced that what He had promised He was also able to perform. And therefore *'it was accounted to him for righteousness.'"*** (Romans 4:20-22) But then the Holy Spirit, speaking through the Apostle Paul, went on to say:

> "Therefore it is of faith that it *might be* according to grace, so that the promise might be sure to all the seed, not only to those who are of the law, but also to those who are of the faith of Abraham, who is the father of us all." (Romans 4:14-16) And, **"Now it was not written for his sake alone that it was imputed to him, but also for us. It shall be imputed to us who believe in Him who raised up Jesus our Lord from the dead, who was delivered up because of our offenses, and was raised because of our justification."** (Romans 4:23-25)

So we see that our God has conditioned even the basic salvation of our souls upon a complete and full reliance upon His faithfulness, upon the fact that we can absolutely rely upon His word. That He will keep absolutely every promise He has ever made. But this brings in a problem. Although He is faithful, we are not faithful. We waffle. Sometimes we come through in a pinch, and sometimes we do not. What about those times? He says **"But the Lord is faithful, who will establish you and guard *you* from the evil one."** (2 Thessalonians 3:3) And **"If we are faithless, He remains faithful; He cannot deny Himself."** (2 Timothy 2:13) He makes provision for our unfaithfulness in two ways. First, He says that:

> "No temptation has overtaken you except such as is common to man; but God is faithful, who will not allow you to be tempted beyond what you are able, but with the temptation will also make the way of escape, that you may be able to bear it." (1 Corinthians 10:13)

And:

> "If we confess our sins, He is faithful and just to forgive us *our* sins and to cleanse us from all unrighteousness." (1 John 1:9)

Again, we see that both of these provisions are based solely upon His own faithfulness, not on any faithfulness on our own part. For we are not reliable. But our God is. He is totally reliable. He will, in all things, do exactly as He said. And this great truth is indeed the very foundation of our faith. Without it, we have nothing.

CHAPTER 5

The Love of God

The scriptures twice say that **"God is love."** (1 John 4:8 and again in 1 John 4:16) They also call Him **"the God of Love"** in 2 Corinthians 13:11. And in the Old Testament, where the name Jehovah, the one true God is usually represented by the word LORD in all capital letters, we find the words **"the LORD loves you"** in Deuteronomy 7:8, **"the LORD your God loves you"** in Deuteronomy 23:5, **"the LORD loves His people"** in 2 Chronicles 2:11, and **"The LORD loves the righteous"** in Psalms 148:6. In addition to this, They also clearly teach that His love is unconquerable. For Paul said:

> "I am persuaded that neither death nor life, nor angels nor principalities nor powers, nor things present nor things to come, nor height nor depth, nor any other created thing, shall be able to separate us from the love of God which is in Christ Jesus our Lord." (Romans 8:38-39)

While the scriptures indeed tell us that our God is a **"God of love,"** And that **"the LORD loves you,"** they also tell us that:

> "In this the love of God was manifested toward us, that God has sent His only begotten Son into the world, that we might live through Him. In this is love, not that we loved God, but that He loved us and sent His Son *to be* the propitiation for our sins." (1 John 4:9-10)

So the proof that God loves us is that He **"sent His only begotten Son into the world, that we might live through Him."** Indeed, this is clearly stated in one of the most well known verses in the entire Bible:

> **"For God so loved the world that He gave His only begotten Son, that whoever believes in Him should not perish but have everlasting life."** (John 3:16)

And we see it again in the words:

> **"But when the kindness and the love of God our Savior toward man appeared, not by works of righteousness which we have done, but according to His mercy He saved us."** (Titus 3:4-5)

Again, we read:

> **"Christ also has loved us and given Himself for us, an offering and a sacrifice to God for a sweet-smelling aroma."** (Ephesians 5:2)

And:

> **"as many as received Him, to them He gave the right to become children of God, to those who believe in His name:"** (John 1:12)

This **"right to become children of God"** is significant to a discussion of the love of God, because the Bible also says:

> **"Behold what manner of love the Father has bestowed on us, that we should be called children of God!"** (1 John 3:1)

Finally, the Lord says:

> "**I love those who love me,**" (Proverbs 8:17)

And Jesus told His disciples that:

> "**the Father Himself loves you, because you have loved Me, and have believed that I came forth from God.**" (John 16:27)

So God is the "**the God of Love**" because "**God is love.**" And "**the LORD your God loves you,**" and proved this by giving "**His only begotten Son.**" And He particularly loves those who love Him, "**because you have loved Me.**" But what about people who spurn His love, and defy Him?

We will see the answer to this question in the next chapter, which is about the justice of God.

CHAPTER 6

The Justice of God

We have been discussing the love of God. But that is only one of His characteristics. Another one is His justice. And although His love is very great, it can never cause Him to ignore His justice, because:

> "Righteousness and justice *are* the foundation of His throne." (Psalm 97:2)

Again, in addressing Him directly, Psalm 89:14 says:

> "Righteousness and justice *are* the foundation of Your throne."

And again, the Bible says,

> "Ascribe greatness to our God.
> *He is* the Rock,
> His work *is* perfect;
> For all His ways *are* justice,
> A God of truth and without injustice;
> Righteous and upright is He." (Deuteronomy 32:3-4)

We need to notice that these scriptures clearly tie righteousness and justice together. Nor are these the only ones that do so. We also read:

> "The LORD executes righteousness And justice for all who are oppressed." (Psalm 103:6) "Also I will make justice the measuring line, And righteousness the plummet; The hail will sweep away the refuge of lies, And the waters will overflow the hiding place." (Isaiah 28:17)

And:

> "The LORD is righteous in her midst, He will do no unrighteousness. Every morning He brings His justice to light; He never fails." (Zephaniah 3:5)

And finally:

> "But the LORD shall endure forever; He has prepared His throne for judgment. He shall judge the world in righteousness, And He shall administer judgment for the peoples in uprightness." (Psalm 9:7-8)

Now why would the Holy Spirit tie these two concepts so closely together, and do it so many times? Men love to imagine that the love of God is too great to allow him to actually punish people in hell. But for a judge to ignore wrongdoing would not be righteousness. In reasoning with the LORD concerning Sodom, Abraham said:

> "Shall not the Judge of all the earth do right?" (Genesis 18:25) But "Sodom and Gomorrah, and the cities around them in a similar manner to these, having given themselves over to sexual immorality and gone after strange flesh, are set forth as an example, suffering the vengeance of eternal fire." (Jude 1:7)

God has warned us in the scriptures about His severe judgment, repeatedly saying such things as:

> "The wicked shall be turned into hell, *And* all the nations that forget God." (Psalm 9:17)

And:

> "Behold, the Lord comes with ten thousands of His saints, to execute judgment on all, to convict all who are ungodly among them of all their ungodly deeds which they have committed in an ungodly way, and of all the harsh things which ungodly sinners have spoken against Him." (Jude 14-15)

Concerning that judgment, He said:

> "Though it tarries, wait for it; Because it will surely come, It will not tarry." (Habakkuk 2:3)

And:

> "For God will bring every work into judgment, Including every secret thing, Whether good or evil." (Ecclesiastes 12:14)

And:

> "Of the increase of *His* government and peace
> There will be no end,
> Upon the throne of David and over His kingdom,
> To order it and establish it with judgment and justice
> From that time forward, even forever.
> The zeal of the LORD of hosts will perform this."
> (Isaiah 9:7)

So let us never imagine that the love of God will block His justice. For He has clearly declared that this will not happen, that His justice will most assuredly be carried out, regardless of His love.

CHAPTER 7

Who is Jesus?

> "In the beginning was the Word, and the Word was with God, and the Word was God. He was in the beginning with God. All things were made through Him, and without Him nothing was made that was made. In Him was life, and the life was the light of men. And the light shines in the darkness, and the darkness did not comprehend it." (John 1:1-5)

In these first five verses of the gospel of John, we see someone called **"the Word,"** who it says **"was with God,"** and also **"was God."** Then, a few verses later, we are told who **"the Word"** is. For it says:

> "And the Word became flesh and dwelt among us, and we beheld His glory, the glory as of the only begotten of the Father, full of grace and truth." (John 1:14)

So we plainly see that this scripture teaches us that **"the Word"** is Jesus. And that both He **"was with God"** and He **"was God."** This sounds like a riddle, but it is not. Instead, it is a part of the doctrine of the Trinity, which we will take up in the next chapter of this book.

And a few chapters after the one we have been discussing, we read of Jesus, that:

> "Therefore the Jews sought all the more to kill Him, because He not only broke the Sabbath, but also said that God was His Father, making Himself equal with God." (John 5:18)

So we see that even the Jews that rejected Jesus understood that in saying **"that God was His Father,"** Jesus was **"making Himself equal with God."** And from the passages we examined in John 1, we understand that saying that Jesus is **"the Son of God"** is equivalent to saying that He is God.

But we need to notice one other detail in the opening verses of John. It says:

> **"All things were made through Him, and without Him nothing was made that was made."** (John 1:3)

That is, this scripture explicitly says that Jesus was the individual that created all things. We see this again in the opening verses of the epistle to the Hebrews.

> **"God, who at various times and in various ways spoke in time past to the fathers by the prophets, has in these last days spoken to us by *His* Son, whom He has appointed heir of all things, through whom also He made the worlds; who being the brightness of *His* glory and the express image of His person, and upholding all things by the word of His power, when He had by Himself purged our sins, sat down at the right hand of the Majesty on high, having become so much better than the angels, as He has by inheritance obtained a more excellent name than they."** (Hebrews 1:1-4)

This passage says, and clearly says, that the Son of God is the one **"through whom also He made the worlds."** But that is not all it says. It clearly also says that He is, even now, **"upholding all things**

by the word of His power." This is why we call Him "the creator and sustainer of the universe."

But the fact that the great Messiah, Jesus, was Divine, was not just revealed after Jesus came. It had been clearly stated long before, by the prophet Isaiah, in the words:

> **"For unto us a Child is born,**
> **Unto us a Son is given;**
> **And the government will be upon His shoulder.**
> **And His name will be called**
> **Wonderful, Counselor, Mighty God,**
> **Everlasting Father, Prince of Peace."** (Isaiah 9:6)

Even the Jews understood this prophecy. For when they put Jesus on trial, they clearly referred to it. For we read that:

> **"Jesus kept silent. And the high priest answered and said to Him, 'I put You under oath by the living God: Tell us if You are the Christ, the Son of God!' Jesus said to him, "It is as you said."** (Matthew 26:63-64)

And Mark 14:61-62 puts it as:

> **"But He kept silent and answered nothing. Again the high priest asked Him, saying to Him, 'Are You the Christ, the Son of the Blessed?' Jesus said, 'I am.'"**

But Jesus did not only state this when He was on trial. The reason they asked this during His trial was because He had clearly said it many other times. The clearest of these is John 8:54, where:

> **"Jesus answered, 'If I honor Myself, My honor is nothing. It is My Father who honors Me, of whom you say that He is your God.'"**

But, as just mentioned, this is not the only time our Lord distinctly stated this. For in John 9, Jesus healed a man who had been born blind, who then testified to the scribes and the pharisees. His testimony angered them so much that they cast him out.

> And **"Jesus heard that they had cast him out; and when He had found him, He said to him, 'Do you believe in the Son of God?' He answered and said, 'Who is He, Lord, that I may believe in Him?' And Jesus said to him, 'You have both seen Him and it is He who is talking with you.'"** (John 9:35-37)

And again we read:

> **"Then they all said, 'Are You then the Son of God?' So He said to them, 'You *rightly* say that I am.'"** (Luke 22:70)

In fact, Jesus called God **"My Father"** 15 times in Matthew, 5 times in Luke, 36 times in John, and 3 times in the Revelation. And God was called **"His Father"** once each in Matthew, Mark, Luke, John, and the Revelation.

This truth is plainly stated in other scriptures as well. Some of these are:

> **"The beginning of the gospel of Jesus Christ, the Son of God."** (Mark 1:1)

And:

> **"For the Son of God, Jesus Christ, who was preached among you by us--by me, Silvanus, and Timothy--was not Yes and No, but in Him was Yes. For all the promises of God in Him *are* Yes, and in Him Amen, to the glory of God through us."** (2 Corinthians 1:19-20)

Two other truths that are closely associated with this, are the fact that Mary was a virgin when Jesus was born, and that He literally rose from the dead. These two doctrines are called "the virgin birth" and "the resurrection." And they are both fundamental doctrines of the Christian faith. Both of these doctrines are important enough to deserve their own chapters in this book. But they are included here because they are so closely linked to the fact that Jesus is indeed the very Son of the Most High God.

If Jesus had been conceived through normal human activity, He would have simply been a normal human being. But He was not a mere human. The fact that he would be born of a virgin had been clearly prophesied hundreds of years earlier, in the words:

> **"Therefore the Lord Himself will give you a sign: Behold, the virgin shall conceive and bear a Son, and shall call His name Immanuel."** (Isaiah 7:14)

Many have objected to the doctrine of "the virgin birth" because the word here translated "virgin" is the softer of the two Hebrew words used for a virgin. The Hebrew word used here is **'alma** (word number 5959 in Strong's Hebrew Dictionary). This word refers to the fact that a young woman is **veiled** or private. And while the word clearly implies that the young woman is a virgin, it does not explicitly say that. But what kind of a **"sign"** would it be for a young woman to get pregnant in the normal way? That happens every day. So the meaning of this sentence is clearly that a **"virgin," "shall conceive and bear a Son,"** and that that virgin birth would be a **"sign."**

And the New Testament clearly states that this is what this prophecy meant. For we read:

> **"Now the birth of Jesus Christ was as follows: After His mother Mary was betrothed to Joseph, before they came together, she was found with child of the Holy Spirit. Then Joseph her husband, being a just** *man*, **and not wanting to make her a public example, was minded to put her away secretly. But while he thought about these**

> things, behold, an angel of the Lord appeared to him in a dream, saying, 'Joseph, son of David, do not be afraid to take to you Mary your wife, for that which is conceived in her is of the Holy Spirit. And she will bring forth a Son, and you shall call His name JESUS, for He will save His people from their sins.' So all this was done that it might be fulfilled which was spoken by the Lord through the prophet, saying: 'Behold, the virgin shall be with child, and bear a Son, and they shall call His name Immanuel,' which is translated, 'God with us.'" (Matthew 1:18-23)

Again:

> "the angel Gabriel was sent by God to a city of Galilee named Nazareth, to a virgin betrothed to a man whose name was Joseph, of the house of David. The virgin's name *was* Mary." (Luke 1:26-27)

And the angel told her:

> "behold, you will conceive in your womb and bring forth a Son, and shall call His name JESUS. He will be great, and will be called the Son of the Highest; and the Lord God will give Him the throne of His father David. And He will reign over the house of Jacob forever, and of His kingdom there will be no end.' Then Mary said to the angel, 'How can this be, since I do not know a man?' And the angel answered and said to her, '*The* Holy Spirit will come upon you, and the power of the Highest will overshadow you; therefore, also, that Holy One who is to be born will be called the Son of God." (Luke 1:31-35)

So we see that the Bible indeed, and very clearly, teaches that Jesus was born of a virgin, and that this proves that He is the **"Son of God."**

And the Bible is just as absolute in insisting upon His literal resurrection. For we read that

> "if Christ is not risen, then our preaching *is* empty and your faith *is* also empty. Yes, and we are found false witnesses of God, because we have testified of God that He raised up Christ, whom He did not raise up--if in fact the dead do not rise. For if *the* dead do not rise, then Christ is not risen. And if Christ is not risen, your faith *is* futile; you are still in your sins!" (1 Corinthians 15:14-17)

So the Holy Spirit clearly teaches that this truth is so critical that if it is not true, we have nothing. For He says that if the Lord Jesus Christ did not rise from the dead, **"our preaching *is* empty and your faith *is* also empty."** And without it **"your faith *is* futile; you are still in your sins!"**

Why is this detail of the gospel so very important? There are two reasons. The first is, as we have seen, that our entire hope of a resurrection, and for a reward in "the afterlife," hangs on ths truth. The second reason is that His resurrection was God's testimony that **"Jesus Christ our Lord"** is indeed **"the Son of God."** This was clearly stated by the Holy Spirit in His introduction to the epistle to the Romans. For that epistle was written:

> "concerning His Son Jesus Christ our Lord, who was born of the seed of David according to the flesh, and declared *to be* the Son of God with power according to the Spirit of holiness, by the resurrection from the dead." (Romans 1:3-4)

So we see that the Holy Spirit himself, speaking through the Apostle Paul, has declared that the resurrection of Christ is indeed a fundamental doctrine of the Christian faith. But why is it fundamental? For two reasons, because the entire hope of our own resurrections hangs on it. But also because this is another proof that **"Jesus Christ our Lord"** is indeed **"the Son of God."**

So what does all this mean to us? Everything! This is a cardinal truth of scripture. For:

> "Whoever confesses that Jesus is the Son of God, God abides in him, and he in God." (1 John 4:15)

There can be no yielding on this truth, for:

> "He who has the Son has life; he who does not have the Son of God does not have life." (1 John 5:12)

And:

> "For God so loved the world that He gave His only begotten Son, that whoever believes in Him should not perish but have everlasting life. For God did not send His Son into the world to condemn the world, but that the world through Him might be saved. He who believes in Him is not condemned; but he who does not believe is condemned already, because he has not believed in the name of the only begotten Son of God." (John 3:16-18)

People imagine that when they "arrive at the pearly gates," a trial will be held, to determine if they should be admitted. But this scripture plainly tells us that the trial has already been held. Whoever **"does not believe is condemned already, because he has not believed in the name of the only begotten Son of God."** So we are offered a simple choice. Believe **"in Him"** and **"have everlasting life."** Or reject Him and find, to your sorrow and eternal loss, that you have been **"condemned already."**

It is critical to understand that if you refuse to believe this, you are not a Christian at all. Regardless of what you call yourself. In that case, you do not have the **"life"** that God speaks of. And sadly, you stand guilty before a holy God, because you have been **"condemned already."**

> "And this is the condemnation, that the light has come into the world, and men loved darkness rather than light, because their deeds were evil." (John 3:19)

CHAPTER 8

The Trinity

The word "Trinity" does not appear anywhere in the Bible. But the concept is there, from its front cover to its back cover.

It appears on the very first page of the Bible where God said:

> **"Let Us make man in Our image, according to Our likeness; let them have dominion over the fish of the sea, over the birds of the air, and over the cattle, over all the earth and over every creeping thing that creeps on the earth."** (Genesis 1:26)

Here, God calls Himself **"Us."** Indeed, the very Hebrew word translated **"God"** throughout the entire Old Testament, is a testimony to the Trinity. For it is plural. In English, adding the sound of the letter S to the end of a word makes it plural. And in Hebrew, adding an M sound to the end of a word does the same thing. In the Hebrew, the word normally translated as **God** is **Elohim**. (This is pronounced like it was spelled El-o-heem, and is word number 430 in Strong's Hebrew Dictionary.) Most of the times you see the word **"God"** in the Old Testament, it is a translation of this plural word. This is even true in Deuteronomy 6:4, where we read, **"Hear, O Israel: The LORD our God, the LORD *is* one."** This literally translates as Hear, O Israel, The LORD our Gods, the LORD is one. This riddle is never explained, even once, anywhere in the entire Old Testament. It is just there. This is just one of many truths that were partly revealed in the Old Testament, but never fully revealed until the New Testament was given.

Another truth that was only partly revealed in the Old Testament was that God has a Son. We find this, for instance, in Proverbs 30:4, which obviously refers to God, and then says, **"What *is* His name, and what *is* his Son's name, if you know?"** And again, Isaiah 7:14 says, **"Behold, the virgin shall conceive and bear a Son, and shall call His name Immanuel."** This name **"Immanuel"** translates literally as **"God with us."** But although such hints as these were included in the Old Testament, even this truth was never fully revealed until the New Testament was given.

Likewise, the **"Spirit of God"** is mentioned many times in the Old Testament, beginning on the first page:

> **"And the Spirit of God was hovering over the face of the waters."** (Genesis 1:2)

In fact, the **"Holy Spirit"** is even named three times in the Old Testament. (Psalms 51:11, Isaiah 63:10, and Isaiah 63:11) But again, none of this was ever clarified until God gave us the New Testament.

But two passages in the New Testament clearly state the three members of the Godhead. The first of these is in the last instruction Jesus gave his disciples, just before He went back to heaven. He said:

> **"Go therefore and make disciples of all the nations, baptizing them in the name of the Father and of the Son and of the Holy Spirit."** (Matthew 28:19)

The other is a passage that some people claim was not actually in the original text of the Bible. But even though many people say this, I reject claims of this type. For they are almost always based on a desire to deny something the Bible teaches, and most of them can be proven to be false. This passage says:

> **"For there are three that bear witness in heaven: the Father, the Word, and the Holy Spirit; and these three are one."** (1 John 5:7)

And John 1:14 shows that **"the Word"** is one of the many scriptural titles of the Lord Jesus. For, as we saw in the last chapter, it says:

> **"And the Word became flesh and dwelt among us, and we beheld His glory, the glory as of the only begotten of the Father, full of grace and truth."**

In the gospels alone (Matthew, Mark, Luke, and John), Jesus called God **"My Father"** more than seventy times. The plainest of these is John 8:54, where Jesus answered:

> **"If I honor Myself, My honor is nothing. It is My Father who honors Me, of whom you say that He is your God."**

So this is clearly two members of the Godhead, **"the Father"** and **"the Son."** So Jesus (the Son) and the Father are distinct persons, even though they are one, as is clearly stated in John 1:1, 10:10, 17:22, and 1 John 5:7.

But now we come to the Holy Spirit. In the New Testament alone, He is called **"the Spirit of God"** twelve times. (Matthew 3:16, 12:28, Romans 8:9, 8:14, 15:19, 1 Corinthians 2:11, 2:14, 3:16, 7:40, 12:3, Ephesians 4:30, and 1 John 4:2) and **"the Spirit of truth"** four times (John 14:17, 15:26, 16:13, and 1 John 4:6.) He is also called **"the Spirit of Grace"** in Hebrews 10:29, **"the Spirit of glory"** in 1 Peter 4:14, and **"the Spirit of holiness"** in Romans 1:4. All these are references to the fact that the Holy Spirit is God, for all these ideas clearly refer to God. But the Holy Spirit is also called **"the Spirit of Christ"** twice (Romans 8:9 and 1 Peter 1:11) and **"the Spirit of Jesus Christ"** in Philippians 1:19, and is also called **"the Spirit of your Father"** in Matthew 10:20. So the Bible clearly tells us that **"the Holy Spirit"** is **"the Spirit of God,"** and also both **"the Spirit of Christ"** and **"the Spirit of the Father."**

But is the Holy Spirit just a spirit that is in both the Father and in the Son? No. He is a distinct person. For he was promised to be sent by the Father in John 14:26 and to be sent by Jesus in John 15:26. Now you cannot "send" yourself. You can "go" somewhere, but that is not "sending yourself." "Sending" someone means either telling or asking someone other than yourself to go somewhere.

So we see that, although the word "Trinity" is not in the Bible, the concept of the Trinity is indeed taught throughout the Bible, and is clearly taught in the New Testament.

CHAPTER 9

Heaven

Most of us have an indistinct concept of heaven as a far off place of bliss, and as the home of God. But what do the scriptures actually tell us about heaven?

We need to consider the actual meanings of the original words used by God, and which are translated **heaven** in our English Bibles.

First, we need to understand that the Biblical word translated **heaven** was either the Hebrew word **shameh**, which is pronounced shaw-meh' and is translated **heaven**, or its plural form **shamayim**. (word number 8064 in Strong's Hebrew Dictionary) In the New Testament, the word translated **heaven** was the Greek word **ouranos**, pronounced oo-ran-os'. (word 3772 in Strong's Greek Dictionary) Both of these words (the Hebrew word and the Greek word) were used in three different senses. Each of these words meant the sky that could be seen in the day time, the blue sky where there are clouds, and where birds fly. They also meant the sky that could be seen at night, when we see beyond the blue to the stars. And they also meant the abode of God. In common usage, it was so easy to see which of these senses was intended, that no specific designation was required. But when it was desired to stress that the meaning was the abode of God, it was called **"the heaven of heavens"** in the Old Testament and **"the third heaven"** in the New Testament. It is similar in our English language, in that the word "heaven" can have any of these same three meanings. But there is a difference between the word **heaven**, as we use it in English, and both the Hebrew and the Greek words that have basically the same meaning. In English, when we simply say **heaven**, we normally mean the abode of God, and other meanings need to be derived from the context. But in both Hebrew and Greek, the normal usage of the word simply meant **the sky**, and other meanings had to be derived from the context.

In the Old Testament we are told very little about heaven, except that it is the abode of God, who is called **"the God of heaven"** eighteen times in the Old Testament, as well as twice in the Revelation, the only book in the New Testament where this term is used. Again the Old Testament refers to **"God in heaven"** seven times, says that **"God is in heaven"** twice, and calls heaven God's habitation five times. But the New Testament does not use any of these three terms. Finally, the scriptures speak many times of God hearing, speaking, or acting **"from heaven."** Most of these are in the Old Testament, but some are in the New.

Before we begin, we need to realize that, contrary to popular opinion, the Bible only **explicitly** speaks of people going to heaven three times, and all of these are exceptional cases. In 2 Kings 2:11 **"Elijah went up by a whirlwind into heaven,"** and in Revelation 11:12 a future event is spoken of, in which the two witnesses whom God will send in the time of the Antichrist, will ascend **"to heaven in a cloud."** And of course, in the first chapter of Acts:

> Jesus **"was taken up, and a cloud received Him out of their sight. And while they looked steadfastly toward heaven as He went up, behold, two men stood by them in white apparel, who also said, 'Men of Galilee, why do you stand gazing up into heaven? This *same* Jesus, who was taken up from you into heaven, will so come in like manner as you saw Him go into heaven.'"** (Acts 1:9-11)

But although the Bible only **explicitly** says this in a few places, and in regard only to exceptional cases, it **very clearly teaches** it in many places.

The first of these we will look at is a very important statement of Jesus himself, when He said:

> "In My Father's house are many mansions; if *it were* not *so*, I would have told you. I go to prepare a place for you. **And if I go and prepare a place for you, I will come again and receive you to Myself; that where I am, *there* you may be also.**" (John 14:2-3)

Here Jesus said He was going away **"to prepare a place for you."** And He made it very clear that this place would be His **"Father's house,"** that is, heaven. And we know that this was indeed where He went:

> "**For Christ has not entered the holy places made with hands, *which are* copies of the true, but into heaven itself, now to appear in the presence of God for us.**" (Hebrews 9:24)

So Jesus went to heaven **"to prepare a place for"** us. But then He said, "**And if I go and prepare a place for you, I will come again and receive you to Myself; that where I am, *there* you may be also.**" It would have been difficult to make this more clear. Jesus went to heaven **"to prepare a place for"** us. And He **"will come again and receive"** us to himself. But why? That we might be with Him. But this speaks of the future. What about the present?

> "**For we know that if our earthly house, *this* tent, is destroyed, we have a building from God, a house not made with hands, eternal in the heavens. For in this we groan, earnestly desiring to be clothed with our habitation which is from heaven, if indeed, having been clothed, we shall not be found naked. For we who are in *this* tent groan, being burdened, not because we want to be unclothed, but further clothed, that mortality may be swallowed up by life. Now He who has prepared us for this very thing is God, who also has given us the Spirit as a guarantee. So *we are* always confident, knowing that while we are at home in the body we are absent from the**

> **Lord. For we walk by faith, not by sight. We are confident, yes, well pleased rather to be absent from the body and to be present with the Lord."** (2 Corinthians 5:1-8)

This scripture clearly tells us that the Christian facing death, the destruction of **"our earthly house, *this* tent,"** has **"a house not made with hands, eternal in the heavens,"** and further, that being **"absent from the body"** is **"to be present with the Lord."** And to put this into the context of going to heaven, we remember that we have already seen many scriptures that make it very plain that our Lord is in heaven, and thus that being present with Him necessarily means being in heaven.

Both Testaments describe myriads surrounding the throne of God. (Daniel 7:10, Revelation 4:2-11) But even in the New Testament, we are told very little about heaven, as the current home of departed saints. As we have seen, we will be with the Lord, and the scriptures clearly say that:

> **"In Your presence is fullness of joy; At Your right hand are pleasures forevermore."** (Psalm 16:11)

So we know that it will be a place of joy in the presence of the Lord. Aside from that, we know very little about the present state of those with the Lord. But we are told a great deal about our future state with Him.

First, we are told that:

> **"it has not yet been revealed what we shall be, but we know that when He is revealed, we shall be like Him, for we shall see Him as He is."** (1 John 3:2)

We can little comprehend what it will be like to **"be like Him."** We can only reflect on this with wonder and awe. Sinless, powerful, and glorious. It is simply beyond our comprehension. **"We shall be like Him!"** This, in and by itself, is enough for any heart in tune with Him today. But there is more. For we read, that:

> "I, John, saw the holy city, New Jerusalem, coming down out of heaven from God, prepared as a bride adorned for her husband. And I heard a loud voice from heaven saying, 'Behold, the tabernacle of God *is* with men, and He will dwell with them, and they shall be His people. God Himself will be with them *and be* their God. And God will wipe away every tear from their eyes; there shall be no more death, nor sorrow, nor crying. There shall be no more pain, for the former things have passed away.' Then He who sat on the throne said, 'Behold, I make all things new.' And He said to me, 'Write, for these words are true and faithful.' And He said to me, 'It is done! I am the Alpha and the Omega, the Beginning and the End. I will give of the fountain of the water of life freely to him who thirsts. He who overcomes shall inherit all things, and I will be his God and he shall be My son.'" (Revelation 21:2-7)

We have already noticed that we have a home **"eternal in the heavens."** But this scripture explicitly says that in that blessed place **"there shall be no more death." "And this is the promise that He has promised us--eternal life."** (1 John 2:25) So from these, as well as from many similar scriptures, we know that our future home will not only be blissful, but eternally blissful.

The city of the saints is described in wondrous words.

> "Then one of the seven angels who had the seven bowls filled with the seven last plagues came to me and talked with me, saying, 'Come, I will show you the bride, the Lamb's wife.' And he carried me away in the Spirit to a great and high mountain, and showed me the great city, the holy Jerusalem, descending out of heaven from God, having the glory of God. Her light *was* like a most precious stone, like a jasper stone, clear as crystal. Also she had a great and high wall with twelve gates, and twelve angels at the gates, and names written on them, which are *the*

names of the twelve tribes of the children of Israel: three gates on the east, three gates on the north, three gates on the south, and three gates on the west. Now the wall of the city had twelve foundations, and on them were the names of the twelve apostles of the Lamb. And he who talked with me had a gold reed to measure the city, its gates, and its wall. The city is laid out as a square; its length is as great as its breadth. And he measured the city with the reed: twelve thousand furlongs. Its length, breadth, and height are equal. Then he measured its wall: one hundred *and* forty-four cubits, *according* to the measure of a man, that is, of an angel. The construction of its wall was *of* jasper; and the city was pure gold, like clear glass. The foundations of the wall of the city *were* adorned with all kinds of precious stones: the first foundation *was* jasper, the second sapphire, the third chalcedony, the fourth emerald, the fifth sardonyx, the sixth sardius, the seventh chrysolite, the eighth beryl, the ninth topaz, the tenth chrysoprase, the eleventh jacinth, and the twelfth amethyst. The twelve gates *were* twelve pearls: each individual gate was of one pearl. And the street of the city *was* pure gold, like transparent glass.

"But I saw no temple in it, for the Lord God Almighty and the Lamb are its temple. The city had no need of the sun or of the moon to shine in it, for the glory of God illuminated it. The Lamb *is* its light. And the nations of those who are saved shall walk in its light, and the kings of the earth bring their glory and honor into it. Its gates shall not be shut at all by day (there shall be no night there). And they shall bring the glory and the honor of the nations into it. But there shall by no means enter it anything that defiles, or causes an abomination or a lie, but only those who are written in the Lamb's Book of Life." (Revelation 21:9-27)

This seems to be symbolic, rather than literal, for the Greek word here translated **furlongs** was **stadios** (word number 4712 in Strong's Greek Dictionary.) As this is thought to have been 607 of our feet, this means that the **"length, breadth, and height"** of the city, were each stated to be one thousand three hundred and eighty miles, or the distance from New York City to Dallas, Texas! Even after reserving slightly over two-thirds of the total volume for structural members and public areas, that would still be large enough to contain a trillion apartments, each one being a 500 foot cube.

But if this description is only symbolic, what must the reality be? Truly, beyond our comprehension. Which would be why the apostle Paul wrote:

> "I know a man in Christ who fourteen years ago— whether in the body I do not know, or whether out of the body I do not know, God knows— such a one was caught up to the third heaven. And I know such a man— whether in the body or out of the body I do not know, God knows— how he was caught up into Paradise and heard inexpressible words, which it is not lawful for a man to utter." (2 Corinthians 12:2-4)

So, whatever is waiting for us, it is so good that it is simply impossible to reduce it into human language.

> "And whoever gives one of these little ones only a cup of cold *water* in the name of a disciple, assuredly, I say to you, he shall by no means lose his reward." (Matthew 10:42)

So from all of this, we know that, for those that have in this life served Christ, there is waiting for them a reward, that this reward will be in a place of indescribable wonder, that it will be pure bliss, and that it will last forever. But the most important part of it all will be that they will be with that Lord whom they so love. And this hope of being **"with the Lord,"** is not just a promise to be fulfilled in some far off time and place, but is something that the saints of God will receive immediately upon leaving their bodies. For we are told in Corinthians 5:8, that:

> **"to be absent from the body"** is **"to be present with the Lord."**

And:

> **"This *hope* we have as an anchor of the soul, both sure and steadfast, and which enters the Presence *behind* the veil."** (Hebrews 6:19)

CHAPTER 10
Hell

As in the case of heaven, we need to notice a little about the Hebrew and Greek words that are translated as **"hell."**

In the Old Testament, the Hebrew word usually translated **hell** was **sheol**, pronounced sheh-ole'. (word number 7585 in Strong's Hebrew Dictionary.) It literally meant **hades**, or the world of the dead. And although this Hebrew word was often translated as **hell**, it actually referred to both the place of punishment and the place of reward.

In the New Testament, the Greek word usually translated **hell** was **geenna**, pronounced gheh'-en-nah. (word number 1067 in Strong's Greek Dictionary) This is often written in English as **ghenna**. It was the name of a valley near Jerusalem where in past days children had been wickedly sacrificed by burning them to death. It was used figuratively by the Jews as a place of eternal punishment. There is a widely circulated report that this was the location of a continually burning rubbish heap just outside of Jerusalem. But there is no record of this claim ever having been made before the time of a Jewish Rabbi named David Kimhi, who is thought to have lived from 1160 to 1235 A.D. So this claim does not have solid historical support.

But the scriptures often say **the pit** in such a way that it clearly means **hell**. In the Old Testament, this is the Hebrew word **shahat**, pronounced shakh'-ath. (word number 7845 in Strong's Hebrew Dictionary) In the New Testament, it is the Greek word **phrear**, pronounced freh'-ar. (word number 5421 in Strong's Greek Dictionary) In the Revelation, this word is repeatedly used with the Greek word **abyssos**, pronounced ab'-us-sos, (word number 12 in Strong's Greek

Dictionary,) which means **bottomless**. So this word combination means "the bottomless pit," which clearly refers to **hell**.

There are also two other Bible words for hell, which have similar looks but completely different meanings. In the Old Testament, the Hebrew word **topteh**, properly pronounced tof-the', (word number 8613 in Strong's Hebrew Dictionary,) which is often written in English as Topheth or sometimes simply Tophet, referred to a place of cremation. But a similar looking New Testament word, **tartaroo**, pronounced tar-tar-o'-o, (word number 5020 in Strong's Greek Dictionary,) being Greek instead of Hebrew, is not even related to **tophet**. This New Testament word is often written in English as Tartarus, and is derived from the name **Tartaros** which in Greek mythology was the deepest abyss of Hades. So Tophet means the place of burning, while Tartarus means the deepest pit of hell.

Finally, **skotos**, pronounced skot'-os (word number 4655 in Strong's Greek Dictionary,) means **darkness**. This word is used symbolically of **evil** generally, and is used for **hell** in combination with the word **outer**, making it **outer darkness**, and in combination with the word **blackness**, in the phrase **the blackness of darkness.**

Hell is also clearly referred to in the New Testament as both the **"lake of fire"** and the **"lake of fire and brimstone,"** and is described as **"eternal fire."** But these words are clear enough that we do not need to examine the Greek.

All these various ways of speaking of hell only highlight the seriousness of God's warnings about the danger of ending up in this horrible place of eternal torment.

We first need to notice that Hell was not prepared for mankind, for Jesus clearly said it was prepared for **"the devil and his angels."** But men will be there. For, in describing the judgment of the nations when He will come, Jesus said that the righteous will be gathered on his right hand, and the wicked on his left. And then He said:

> **"Then He will also say to those on the left hand, 'Depart from Me, you cursed, into the everlasting fire prepared for the devil and his angels:'"** (Matthew 25:41)

Again, Jesus said:

> **"It is better for you to enter into life lame or maimed, than having two hands or two feet, to be cast into the everlasting fire."** (Matthew 18:8)

So we see that hell is not only a place of **"fire,"** but of **"everlasting fire."**

Many are quite willing to think of everlasting reward in heaven, but cannot accept the concept of everlasting punishment in hell. They imagine that a loving God would never do such a thing as to torment even the worst of people for ever. But this involves two false concepts. The first of these is a false concept of God. For God is not only a God of love, but also God of justice. The other false concept is that of guilt. For even the best of mankind is far more evil than we can imagine. Indeed, scripture tells us that:

> **"The heart is deceitful above all *things*, And desperately wicked; Who can know it?"** (Jeremiah 17:9)

Concerning such reasonings of men, God's answer is:

> **"But indeed, O man, who are you to reply against God?"** (Romans 9:20)

When divinely confronted about his error in complaining about the ways of God, Job repented and answered:

> **"I have uttered what I did not understand, Things too wonderful for me, which I did not know."** (Job 42:3)

And those who so complain today would indeed do well to learn from Job's example.

Scripture could hardly be more clear in teaching that the punishment for sin will be eternal torment. For concerning three individuals who had been **"cast into the lake of fire and brimstone,"** we read:

> **"And they will be tormented day and night forever and ever."** (Revelation 20:10)

And this same verse says, concerning two of these three individuals, that this is where **"the beast and the false prophet *are*."** This is significant because it had been a full thousand years earlier that:

> **"These two were cast alive into the lake of fire burning with brimstone."** (Revelation 19:20)

For the Millennium had taken place between these two events. (Revelation 20:1-7)

Again, we read concerning **"the men Who have transgressed against Me"** that **"their worm does not die, And their fire is not quenched."** (Isaiah 66:24) And Jesus cited this scripture three times over, saying, **"where *Their worm does not die, And the fire is not quenched.*"** (Mark 9:44, 46, and 48) So we see that, even as the redeemed will live forever in heaven, the rest will also live forever, but in torment. We have already noticed that this is called **"everlasting fire"** in Matthew 18:8 and 25:41. It is also called **"eternal fire"** in Jude 7. Some have made the excuse that just because the fire is eternal does not mean that the people who are sent there will be there forever. They want to think that those condemned to this fire will simply be consumed, and will cease to exist. We have already examined scriptures that clearly show that this is not correct. But lest anyone doubt the meaning, this is also called **"eternal condemnation"** in Mark 3:29, **"eternal Judgment"** in Hebrews 6:2, and **"everlasting punishment"** in Matthew 25:46. It is also called the **"everlasting home"** of both evil spirits and evil men in Luke 16:9.

But who will receive this eternal punishment? We read of the final judgment:

> **"Then Death and Hades were cast into the lake of fire. This is the second death. And anyone not found written in the Book of Life was cast into the lake of fire."** (Revelation 20:14-15)

What is this **"Book of Life"**? It is mentioned seven times in scripture. (Philippians 4:3 and Revelation 3:5, 13:8, 17:8, 20:12, and 15, and 21:27.) The sum total of all these references is that **"the Book of life"** is the Lord's record of all those who are His own. This is very clear in the last place where it is mentioned. For in speaking of **"the bride, the Lamb's wife"** which was depicted as **"the great city, the holy Jerusalem,"** (Revelation 21:9-10) the Holy Spirit said:

> **"there shall by no means enter it anything that defiles, or causes an abomination or a lie, but only those who are written in the Lamb's Book of Life."** (Revelation 21:27) But, as we have seen, **"anyone not found written in the Book of Life was cast into the lake of fire."** (Revelation 20:14-15)

So we see that our Lord has decreed this eternal punishment for everyone who is not one of His own. That is, everyone who is not **"washed"** from their **"sins,"** **"in His own blood."** (Revelation 1:5)

There is also a distinct difference between the place where sinners are currently held in torment, and their permanent abode in **"the lake of fire."** The Greek name of the current place is **Hades**, pronounced hah'-dace. (word number 86 in Strong's Greek Dictionary) In our translation this word is transliterated as **Hades**, but in others it is usually rendered **hell**. In a sense, these other translations are correct, as the word **hell** has come to simply mean an indistinct place of torment. But, technically speaking, **"Hades"** and **"the lake of fire"** are different places. We know this because **"Hades"** will be **"cast into the lake of fire."** (Revelation 20:14)

There are also other scriptures that make this clear. One of these is the anecdote of the rich man and Lazarus. This is usually called a parable. But that is an error. For a parable is a fictitious story told to illustrate a point, while an anecdote is a short factual account. And Jesus did not tell this story with any of the typical language of parables, such as **"is like."** He simply stated it as a factual account. And after describing the lives of the rich man and Lazarus, Jesus said:

> **"So it was that the beggar died, and was carried by the angels to Abraham's bosom. The rich man also died and was buried. And being in torments in Hades, he lifted up his eyes and saw Abraham afar off, and Lazarus in his bosom. Then he cried and said, 'Father Abraham, have mercy on me, and send Lazarus that he may dip the tip of his finger in water and cool my tongue; for I am tormented in this flame.' But Abraham said, 'Son, remember that in your lifetime you received your good things, and likewise Lazarus evil things; but now he is comforted and you are tormented. And besides all this, between us and you there is a great gulf fixed, so that those who want to pass from here to you cannot, nor can those from there pass to us.'"** (Luke 16:22-26)

We need to notice that, although the rich man and Lazarus were respectively in places of torment and of comfort, they could both see and communicate with each other. But at the same time they could not pass over the **"great gulf"** that was **"fixed"** between them. This is significantly different from the **"holy city"** of Revelation 20:2, 19 and both the **"outer darkness"** of Matthew 8:12, 22:13 and 25:30, and the **"bottomless pit"** mentioned in Revelation 9:1, 2, 11, 11;7, 17:8, and 20:1, and 3.

What, then, do we know about hell? It is a place of torment, it is an eternal fire, in which souls suffer but do not die. And thus, the torment will last forever, for there is no way to pass over to the regions of bliss. It is a place of darkness. And it is the place into which **"the wicked shall be turned,"** along with **"all the nations that forget God."**

How critical, then, is it, to, at all costs, avoid ever ending up in this horrible place of eternal torment. But everyone, without a single exception, is already condemned to this awful fate unless they have turned to the Lord Jesus Christ in faith and repentance, and given up all hope of ever deserving anything but punishment. This, as we have seen, is not just the opinions of mere men, but the clear and unequivocal declaration of the word of God, the Bible.

For here is what Jesus himself actually said about this:

> **"For God so loved the world that He gave His only begotten Son, that whoever believes in Him should not perish but have everlasting life. For God did not send His Son into the world to condemn the world, but that the world through Him might be saved. He who believes in Him is not condemned; <u>but he who does not believe is condemned already, because he has not believed in the name of the only begotten Son of God. And this is the condemnation, that the light has come into the world, and men loved darkness rather than light, because their deeds were evil."</u>** (John 3:16-19)

And we read:

> "There were present at that season some who told Him about the Galileans whose blood Pilate had mingled with their sacrifices. And Jesus answered and said to them, 'Do you suppose that these Galileans were worse sinners than all *other* Galileans, because they suffered such things? I tell you, no; but <u>unless you repent you will all likewise perish. Or those eighteen on whom the tower in Siloam fell and killed them, do you think that they were worse sinners than all</u> other men who dwelt in Jerusalem? <u>I tell you, no; but unless you repent you will all likewise perish.'"</u> (Luke 13:1-5)

So here we see, clearly stated by Jesus Himself, that **"he who does not believe is condemned already,"** and that **"unless you repent you shall all likewise perish."** These are not the words of mere men, but of the Lord Jesus Christ Himself, who is the great Judge before whom every man shall one day stand. I plead with and implore anyone and everyone who reads or hears this, to heed this warning while they still have time.

CHAPTER 11

Our Guilt Before God

We can never even begin to understand our spiritual condition, or the justice of God's condemnation of all mankind, until we realize our guilt before God. The Bible says that:

> "Most men will proclaim each his own goodness, But who can find a faithful man?" (Proverbs 20:6)

And it also says:

> "But they, measuring themselves by themselves, and comparing themselves among themselves, are not wise." (2 Corinthians 10:12)

The truth of these scriptures was graphically demonstrated to me many years ago when, within the space of a few months, I had a drug dealer boast to me that he had never stolen anything in his life, a professional thief boast to me that he had never sold drugs, and a third man tell me that he was "basically a good man," if it were not for the fact that he was "such a bloody murderer!" That is, each of these unusually wicked people still proclaimed their own goodness, and did so on the basis of their imagination of how they compared to other people. But God says this is not wise. And the gross foolishness of this type of thinking was starkly demonstrated in a man imagining that he was still "basically a good man," even though he admitted he was "such a bloody murderer."

Instead of comparing ourselves with other people, we need to compare ourselves to God. And when we do that, we suddenly realize that we simply do not measure up. But why do we need to use such a harsh standard? Because the one who is going to judge us is God. And God does not grade on a curve. We therefore need to consider what God, the Righteous Judge, says about us. That is, about each of us, as individuals. So what does God say?

> **"As it is written: 'There is none righteous, no, not one; There is none who understands; There is none who seeks after God. They have all turned aside; They have together become unprofitable; There is none who does good, no, not one.' 'Their throat is an open tomb; With their tongues they have practiced deceit'; 'The poison of asps is under their lips'; 'Whose mouth is full of cursing and bitterness.' 'Their feet are swift to shed blood; Destruction and misery are in their ways; And the way of peace they have not known.' 'There is no fear of God before their eyes.'"** (Romans 3:10-18)

So this scripture makes it very plain. In the opinion of God (and, since He is the Ultimate Judge, his opinion is the only one that counts,) **"There is none who does good, no, not one."** This pronouncement from the Judge of all the universe, leaves no wiggle room. We are all condemned. There are no exceptions. For God's standard is:

> **"you shall be perfect, just as your Father in heaven is perfect."** (Matthew 5:48)

Again, we are told that:

> **"the LORD saw that the wickedness of man *was* great in the earth, and *that* every intent of the thoughts of his heart *was* only evil continually."** (Genesis 6:5) And, **"we are all like an unclean thing, And all our righteousnesses are like filthy rags."** (Isaiah 64:6)

So we are all guilty. Even the great David prayed:

> **"Do not enter into judgment with Your servant, For in Your sight no one living is righteous."** (Psalm 143:2)

We understand God's judgment in this regard a little better when we consider these words of Jesus:

> **"You have heard that it was said to those of old, *You shall not murder*, and whoever murders will be in danger of the judgment.' But I say to you that whoever is angry with his brother without a cause shall be in danger of the judgment. And whoever says to his brother, 'Raca!'** [1] **shall be in danger of the council. But whoever says, 'You fool!' shall be in danger of hell fire."** (Matthew 5:21-22)

So, as we are told in another scripture:

> **"*the Lord does* not see as man sees; for man looks at the outward appearance, but the LORD looks at the heart."** (1 Samuel 16:7) And our Lord himself said, **"You have heard that it was said to those of old, *'You shall not commit adultery.'* But I say to you that whoever looks at a woman to lust for her has already committed adultery with her in his heart."** (Matthew 5:27-28)

In spite of all this, many people will still say that they have not sinned. To this, God answers:

> **"If we say that we have no sin, we deceive ourselves, and the truth is not in us."** (1 John 1:8)

---

1   "Raca" was a Jewish term of utter contempt, literally meaning 'empty one.' It was their equivalent of one of us calling someone a "worthless piece of trash."

Others will say that they are not aware of any sin in their lives. So what does God say about this? Very few of us would compare ourselves to the great Apostle Paul. But even he said:

> "I know nothing against myself, yet I am not justified by this; but He who judges me is the Lord." (1 Corinthians 4:4)

And David prayed:

> "Who can understand *his* errors? Cleanse me from secret *faults*." (Psalm 19:12)

The basic principle that applies to this claim is stated in the law of Moses, saying:

> "If a person sins, and commits any of these things which are forbidden to be done by the commandments of the LORD, though he does not know *it*, yet he is guilty and shall bear his iniquity." (Leviticus 5:17)

But our problem is not only our guilt, but our inability to do anything to get rid of it. For God himself said:

> "though you wash yourself with lye, and use much soap, *Yet* your iniquity is marked before Me," says the Lord GOD." (Jeremiah 2:22)

People want to proclaim their own "good works," and imagine that these will be accepted by God. But God's answer is that:

> "by the deeds of the law no flesh will be justified in His sight, for by the law is the knowledge of sin." (Romans 3:20)

And again, He says:

> **"for by the works of the law no flesh shall be justified."**
> Galatians 2:16)

No such things will be accepted by God. But He has made provision for our guilt, which provision is the subject of a later chapter of this book.

CHAPTER 12

The Need for Repentance

There is a fundamental part of the gospel that has often been overlooked. That part, which, as we noticed, is indeed fundamental, is repentance. The gospel is not just "believe in Jesus," but "repent, and believe in Jesus." Indeed God says:

> "**You believe that there is one God. You do well. Even the demons believe – and tremble!**" (James 2:19)

In other words, God says, "Oh! So you believe in God? You're doing good. SO DOES THE DEVIL!"

Again, we read:

> "There were present at that season some who told Him about the Galileans whose blood Pilate had mingled with their sacrifices. And Jesus answered and said to them, 'Do you suppose that these Galileans were worse sinners than all *other* Galileans, because they suffered such things? I tell you, no; but unless you repent you will all likewise perish. Or those eighteen on whom the tower in Siloam fell and killed them, do you think that they were worse sinners than all *other* men who dwelt in Jerusalem? I tell you, no; but unless you repent you will all likewise perish.'" (Luke 13:1-5)

The word of God says:

> "though you wash yourself with lye, and use much soap, Yet your iniquity is marked before Me." (Jeremiah 2:22)

So we cannot wash away our guilt, and we will see that neither good works nor great contributions will remove it. In short, we can do nothing about our guilt. We will also see that our God can remove this guilt. But He puts a condition on this removal.

When Jesus first began to preach, his message was:

> "Repent, and believe in the gospel." (Mark 1:15)

And a little later He said:

> "I have not come to call *the* righteous, but sinners, to repentance." (Luke 5:32)

And a few years later, God said through the Apostle Paul:

> "Truly, these times of ignorance God overlooked, but now commands all men everywhere to repent." (Acts 17:30)

But real repentance always produces confession. So God says:

> "Only acknowledge your iniquity, That you have transgressed against the LORD your God." (Jeremiah 3:13)

And David said:

> "I acknowledged my sin to You, And my iniquity I have not hidden. I said, 'I will confess my transgressions to the LORD,' And You forgave the iniquity of my sin." (Psalm 32:5)

This is why the Holy Spirit says:

> **"If we confess our sins, He is faithful and just to forgive us *our* sins and to cleanse us from all unrighteousness."** (1 John 1:9)

So we see that the Bible clearly teaches two complementary concepts, that every one of us is guilty before God, and that He demands that we repent. And along the way, It also warns us that we can neither wash our guilt away, nor atone for it with either good works or with contributions to worthy causes. Instead, He demands that we:

> **"repent, and believe the gospel."** (Mark 1:15)

Nothing else will avail. And without this, all hope is vain. For **"unless you repent you will all likewise perish."**

CHAPTER 13

God's Provision for Our Guilt

When people realize their guilt before God, their common reaction is to consider how they can make amends for their sins. They want to "do" something to "make it up" to God for all their sins. But the scriptures very clearly say that:

> "**not by works of righteousness which we have done, but according to His mercy He saved us.**" (Titus 3:5)

And:

> "**by grace you have been saved through faith, and that not of yourselves;** *it is* **the gift of God, not of works, lest anyone should boast.**" (Ephesians 2:8-9)

But it is not only true that good deeds that will not avail. Gifts, that is, contributions to worthy causes, are also useless in this regard. For:

> "**you were not redeemed with corruptible things,** *like* **silver or gold, from your aimless conduct** *received* **by tradition from your fathers, but with the precious blood of Christ, as of a lamb without blemish and without spot.**" (1 Peter 1:18-19)

So if God will accept neither good works nor great contributions, what will He accept? We might well ask, with ancient Job:

> "how can a man be righteous before God?" (Job 9:2)

Our God has told us that:

> "without shedding of blood there is no remission." (Hebrews 9:22)

And that:

> "it *is* the blood *that* makes atonement for the soul." (Leviticus 17:11)

So it is clear that blood is needed. But what blood? We need to go back to the passage in 1 Peter that we just considered:

> "you were not redeemed with corruptible things, like silver or gold, from your aimless conduct received by tradition from your fathers, but with the precious blood of Christ, as of a lamb without blemish and without spot." (1 Peter 1:18-19)

We first considered this passage in the light of what God would not receive, but now we need to notice what it says He will receive. For it says that they had been redeemed **"with the precious blood of Christ, as of a lamb without blemish and without spot."** So we are redeemed **"with the precious blood of Christ."** In the law of Moses they had been told that:

"it is the blood *that* makes atonement for the soul." (Leviticus 17:11)

"And according to the law almost all things are purified with blood, and without shedding of blood there is no remission." (Hebrews 9:22)

"But Christ came *as* High Priest of the good things to come, with the greater and more perfect tabernacle not made with hands, that is, not of this creation. Not with the blood of goats and calves, but with His own blood He entered the Most Holy Place once for all, having obtained eternal redemption. For if the blood of bulls and goats and the ashes of a heifer, sprinkling the unclean, sanctifies for the purifying of the flesh, how much more shall the blood of Christ, who through the eternal Spirit offered Himself without spot to God, cleanse your conscience from dead works to serve the living God?" (Hebrews 9:11-14) So the blood that Christ offered at Calvary is the blood that God demands for the cleansing of our guilt. This is God's provision for our guilt, and it is the only provision He will accept. For we read that **"He who has the Son has life; he who does not have the Son of God does not have life."** (1 John 5:12) And **"For God so loved the world that He gave His only begotten Son, that whoever believes in Him should not perish but have everlasting life. For God did not send His Son into the world to condemn the world, but that the world through Him might be saved. He who believes in Him is not condemned; but he who does not believe is condemned already, because he has not believed in the name of the only begotten Son of God."** (John 3:16-18)

But the blood of Christ was shed not only **"as of a lamb,"** but **"as of a lamb without blemish and without spot."** Why is this? Because our Lord Jesus, who gave himself for us at Calvary:

> "'*committed no sin, Nor was deceit found in His mouth*'; who, when He was reviled, did not revile in return; when He suffered, He did not threaten, but committed *Himself* to Him who judges righteously; who Himself bore our sins in His own body on the tree." (1 Peter 2:22-24)
>
> "For He made Him who knew no sin *to be* sin for us." (2 Corinthians 5:21)
>
> "And you know that He was manifested to take away our sins, and in Him there is no sin." (1 John 3:5)

The fact that our Lord Jesus was sinless is why the angel, in telling Mary that He would be born, called Jesus **"Holy,"** saying, **"that Holy One who is to be born will be called the Son of God."** (Luke 1:35) So the fact that the lamb had to be **"without blemish and without spot,"** spoke of the sinless perfection of our Lord Jesus Christ:

> who "*was* wounded for our transgressions, *He was* bruised for our iniquities; The chastisement for our peace *was* upon Him, And by His stripes we are healed. All we like sheep have gone astray; We have turned, every one, to his own way; And the LORD has laid on Him the iniquity of us all." (Isaiah 53:5-6)

How could our hearts not be moved by the greatness of the provision God has made for our guilt? That He, the God of all the universe, would give His own only and dearly beloved Son, as a sacrifice to atone for our sins! But what of anyone who despises this great provision?

> "Anyone who has rejected Moses' law dies without mercy on the testimony of two or three witnesses. Of how much worse punishment, do you suppose, will he be thought worthy who has trampled the Son of God underfoot, counted the blood of the covenant by which he was sanctified a common thing, and insulted the Spirit of grace? For we know Him who said, '*Vengeance is Mine, I*

> *will repay,'* says the Lord. And again, *'The LORD will judge His people.'* It is a fearful thing to fall into the hands of the living God." (Hebrews 10:28-31)

So the question each one of us must face is, will I accept the provision God has made for my guilt, or will I invent some other imagined provision of my own. Your eternity hangs in the balance. What will you choose?

CHAPTER 14

The Need to be Born Again

When Nicodemus, a Pharisee who was a ruler of the Jews, came to Jesus by night, Jesus told him:

> **"Most assuredly, I say to you, unless one is born again, he cannot see the kingdom of God."** (John 3:4)

Like many modern men, Nicodemus was perplexed by this, so:

> **"Nicodemus said to Him, 'How can a man be born when he is old? Can he enter a second time into his mother's womb and be born?' Jesus answered, 'Most assuredly, I say to you, unless one is born of water and the Spirit, he cannot enter the kingdom of God. That which is born of the flesh is flesh, and that which is born of the Spirit is spirit. Do not marvel that I said to you, "You must be born again." The wind blows where it wishes, and you hear the sound of it, but cannot tell where it comes from and where it goes. So is everyone who is born of the Spirit.' "** (John 3:5-8)

This process of being **"born again,"** is the process by which a person is transformed from being a child of the devil into being a child of God. Many people say, "We are all God's children," and imagine that the Bible teaches this. But indeed, it teaches the very opposite, saying:

> **"In this the children of God and the children of the devil are manifest: Whoever does not practice righteousness is not of God, nor *is* he who does not love his brother."** (1 John 3:10)

In fact, Jesus went so far as to explicitly say to some:

> **"You are of *your* father the devil,"** (John 8:44)

So we need to realize that the scriptures do NOT say that "we all are God's children."

Indeed, one of the most misused scriptures in the entire Bible is:

> **"For you are all sons of God through faith in Christ Jesus."** (Galatians 3:26)

Many stress the first part of this verse, without noticing the last part. For we only become **"sons of God," "through faith in Christ Jesus."** As Jesus himself said another place:

> **"But as many as received Him, to them He gave the right to become children of God, to those who believe in His name: who were born, not of blood, nor of the will of the flesh, nor of the will of man, but of God."** (John 1:12-13)

You cannot **"become"** something you already are, and you cannot be given a **"right"** which you already have. But this **"right to become children of God"** is only given to **"as many as received Him."** The rest, sadly, remain **"the children of the devil."**

Christians are exhorted to love one another:

> **"having been born again, not of corruptible seed but incorruptible, through the word of God which lives and abides forever."** (1 Peter 1:23)

From the scriptures we have examined we learn three things about the new birth. First we saw that this term refers to a spiritual birth. Then we learned that this is a **"right"** which is given to **"as many as received Him"** and **"to those who believe in His name,"** and finally, that it comes **"through the word of God."** So this new birth, being **"born again,"** is a transformation that takes place within an individual when they choose to believe in the name of the Lord Jesus Christ, about whom they learned **"through the word of God."** At that time, each individual believer is **"born, not of blood, nor of the will of the flesh, nor of the will of man, but of God."**

This process of becoming a child of God is also called being **"adopted"** by God. Rather than being a different process, this is just a different aspect of this same process, the process by which **"children of the devil"** become **"children of God."**

The **"born again"** aspect of this process refers to a radical change that occurs in people when they become **"children of God,"** as we read in 2 Corinthians 5:17:

> "Therefore, if anyone is in Christ, *he is* a new creation; old things have passed away; behold, all things have become new."

This is a change from being **"by nature children of wrath,"** (Ephesians 2:3) to being **"partakers of the divine nature."** (2 Peter 1:4) And it is called being changed from **"the old man"** into **"the new man"** in both Ephesians 4:22-24 and Colossians 3:9-10.

But the **"adoption"** aspect of this process does not refer to the change in our natures which occurs at the time we believe, but to the change in our relationship with God which takes place at that time. The first place we read about this **"adoption"** is:

> "But when the fullness of the time had come, God sent forth His Son, born of a woman, born under the law, to redeem those who were under the law, that we might receive the adoption as sons. And because you are sons, God has sent forth the Spirit of His Son into your hearts,

> crying out, 'Abba, Father!' Therefore you are no longer a slave but a son, and if a son, then an heir of God through Christ." (Galatians 4:4-7) And again we are told, "**Blessed be** the God and Father of our Lord Jesus Christ, who has blessed us with every spiritual blessing in the heavenly *places* in Christ, just as He chose us in Him before the foundation of the world, that we should be holy and without blame before Him in love, having predestined us to adoption as sons by Jesus Christ to Himself, according to the good pleasure of His will, to the praise of the glory of His grace, by which He has made us accepted in the Beloved." (Ephesians 1:3-6)

So the **"adopted"** aspect of this change which occurs when we believe in the Lord Jesus Christ, is the change in which a man becomes **"no longer a slave but a son, and if a son, then an heir of God through Christ."** And in which **"He has made us accepted in the Beloved."** Indeed:

> **"Behold what manner of love the Father has bestowed on us, that we should be called children of God!"** (1 John 3:1)

In the Holy Scriptures, this process is also called being saved, as we read in Acts 16:31:

> **"Believe on the Lord Jesus Christ, and you will be saved."** And in John 3:16-17, where we also read, **"For God so loved the world that He gave His only begotten Son, that whoever believes in Him should not perish but have everlasting life. For God did not send His Son into the world to condemn the world, but that the world through Him might be saved."**

This aspect of this process refers to the rescue of believers from the punishment for their many sins. God can righteously do this because our Lord Jesus **"bore our sins in His own body on the tree"** (1 Peter 2:24) So that:

> **"by Him everyone who believes is justified from all things."** (Acts 13:39)

And:

> **"Blessed are those whose lawless deeds are forgiven, And whose sins are covered; Blessed is the man to whom the LORD shall not impute sin."** (Romans 4:7-8)

CHAPTER 15

The Need for Good Works

We have seen that good works have no part in salvation. That is, in the removal of our guilt before God. Our salvation is based on the blood of Christ, and the blood of Christ alone. And it is obtained through faith. That is, it is obtained through belief in what God has said about the cleansing power of that blood. But this does not mean that good works are not necessary. The truth is, that in every place where the Bible says that good works will not save us, within a few verses it also says they are needed. For a heart that is filled with God's love will flow out in good works of every kind. For we read that:

> "the fruit of the Spirit is love, joy, peace, longsuffering, kindness, goodness, faithfulness, gentleness, self-control." (Galatians 5:22-23)

But this is not only the natural result of a heart filled with God's love. It is a requirement for His service. For the Holy Spirit said:

> "This is a faithful saying, and these things I want you to affirm constantly, that those who have believed in God should be careful to maintain good works. These things are good and profitable to men." (Titus 3:8)

This is not just a concept that is stated in a few places in scripture, but is taught again and again, in words such as:

> "And let our people also learn to maintain good works, to meet urgent needs, that they may not be unfruitful." (Titus 3:14)

And:

> "Therefore do not let sin reign in your mortal body, that you should obey it in its lusts. And do not present your members *as* instruments of unrighteousness to sin, but present yourselves to God as being alive from the dead, and your members as instruments of righteousness to God." (Romans 6:12-13)

Indeed, the scriptures tell us that this is one of the purposes of our salvation. For in speaking of Christ, we read:

> "who Himself bore our sins in His own body on the tree, that we, having died to sins, might live for righteousness--by whose stripes you were healed." (1 Peter 2:24)

And:

> "For He made Him who knew no sin *to be* sin for us, that we might become the righteousness of God in Him." (2 Corinthians 5:21)

And again:

> "For we are His workmanship, created in Christ Jesus for good works, which God prepared beforehand that we should walk in them." (Ephesians 2:10)

And again we read:

> "For the grace of God that brings salvation has appeared to all men, teaching us that, denying ungodliness and worldly lusts, we should live soberly, righteously, and godly in the present age, looking for the blessed hope and glorious appearing of our great God and Savior Jesus Christ, who gave Himself for us, that He might redeem us from every lawless deed and purify for Himself His own special people, zealous for good works." (Titus 2:11-14)

And again, the Holy Spirit said through Paul:

> "Awake to righteousness, and do not sin; for some do not have the knowledge of God. I speak *this* to your shame." (1 Corinthians 15:34)

And:

> "Flee also youthful lusts; but pursue righteousness, faith, love, peace with those who call on the Lord out of a pure heart." (2 Timothy 2:22)

And:

> "But you, O man of God, flee these things and pursue righteousness, godliness, faith, love, patience, gentleness." (1 Timothy 6:11)

And finally we read that:

> "In this the children of God and the children of the devil are manifest: Whoever does not practice righteousness is not of God, nor is he who does not love his brother." (1 John 3:10)

So, while good works have no part in salvation, they are indeed a necessary part of the Christian life. So much so that a lack of them shows that a person is not really a Christian.

> For **"He who says, 'I know Him,' and does not keep His commandments, is a liar, and the truth is not in him."** (1 John 2:4)

CHAPTER 16
Eternal Security

There are many sincere Christians, who deeply love the Lord Jesus Christ, but do not understand this critical concept. And many of these would be very offended at the suggestion that this is a fundamental doctrine of the Christian faith. But regardless of the opinions of anyone, this is indeed taught in the scriptures, and not only taught, but insisted upon, and not only insisted upon, but insisted upon as a basic and fundamental doctrine.

Many have the notion that after we die, there will be a trial held to see if we will be admitted to heaven, to see if we have been "good enough." But this is a serious mistake. For the trial has already been held. And all have been already condemned. For the word of God plainly says that:

> "**He who believes in Him is not condemned; but he who does not believe is condemned already, because he has not believed in the name of the only begotten Son of God.**" (John 3:18)

But there is a widespread second error, which is really only a modification of this error, that after we **have already been** saved by trusting Jesus, we need to do something to **stay** saved. The people who have been deceived by this idea fail to realize that they can no more deserve to **stay** saved, than they had deserved to **become** saved in the first place. We need to realize that **everything** is based on the holy blood shed for us at Calvary. We need to consider the very words of Jesus:

> "Most assuredly, I say to you, he who hears My word and believes in Him who sent Me has everlasting life, and shall not come into judgment, but has passed from death into life." (John 5:24)

I particularly love how the Contemporary English Version renders this verse.

> "I tell you for certain that everyone who hears my message and has faith in the one who sent me has eternal life and will never be condemned. They have already gone from death to life." (John 5:24, CEV)

So we see that, for the believer, as for the unbeliever, the trial has already been held. **"Everyone"** who has this faith **"will never be condemned."** And why? Because **"They have already gone from death to life."**

But we also need to notice the explicit wording of both of these translations, that whoever believes **"has"** an unending life. The Greek word here translated **has** is **echei.** (a form of word number 2192 in Strong's Greek Dictionary) It indicates present possession, not future possession. That is, the meaning of the Greek words used here, is that whoever hears the words of Jesus and believes in Him that sent Him, **already has** life. And that this life will never end. That is the real, literal, meaning of the Greek words used in this passage. And then, this is reinforced with the promise that such a person will never be condemned.

But we need to consider the basic meaning of the words **"everlasting life,"** as rendered in the first translation above, or **"eternal life,"** as rendered in the other. In this regard, we need to realize that any life that has been lost was **never "everlasting,"** or **"eternal."** For by its very definition, such a life cannot ever end. **"Everlasting life,"** or **"eternal life,"** neither means nor implies a life that has **the potential** to last for ever. Instead, it means a life that **will** last forever. That is, that it **cannot** be lost. And that is what Jesus meant when He said:

> "as Moses lifted up the serpent in the wilderness, even so must the Son of Man be lifted up, that whoever believes in Him should not perish but have eternal life. For God so loved the world that He gave His only begotten Son, that whoever believes in Him should not perish but have everlasting life." (John 3:14-16)

But here we also need to consider the word **"believes"** that occurs in four places in the passages we have just examined. (John 3:18, 5:24, 3:15, and 3:16) and is rendered as **"has faith"** in the CEV version of John 5:24. The Greek word translated this way is **pisteuon,** a present active form of the Greek word **pisteuo**, word number 4100 in Strong's Greek Dictionary. We need to notice this because some people claim that this form of this Greek word means "keeps on believing." But that is not what it means.

As the explanation of why this claim is incorrect is complicated, and involves a somewhat technical analysis of the Greek text, this explanation has been put in a footnote, so anyone who is intimidated by such a long and technical explanation, or who is simply not interested, can easily just skip over it.[2]

---

[2] It is indeed true that the Greek present tense indicates continued action, something that happens continually or repeatedly. But it can also indicate only something that is in the process of happening. And in these cases, as in all interpretation of scripture, or even for that matter, of any literature of any kind, the context in which a word is used is critical to its correct interpretation. Words do not stand alone. They relate to each other. So we always have to consider the context in which they are used. And in each of the places we are discussing, (John 3:18, 5:24, 3:15, and 3:16) The context is the present.

We see this in the words **"is not condemned"** in John 3:18. In the Greek, this is **ou krinetai** the word **ou** means "not" and the word **krinetai** is a present indicative form of the Greek word **krino**, word number 2919 in Strong's Greek Dictionary, which in this context means condemned. But in Greek, a present indicative verb describes an action that is taking place at the present time. So this means that the context of the present active form of "believing" indicates that it has the alternate meaning of only something that is in the process of happening at the present time, as mentioned above, rather than something that must keep on happening.

We see this again the words **"has everlasting life"** in John 5:24. As we have already noticed, the Greek word translated "has" is **echei**. But we did not take notice of the fact that, as in the words translated **"is not condemned"** in John 3:18, the word **echei** is a present indicative form of the Greek word **echo**, word number 2192 in Strong's Greek Dictionary. So the context of the word

Again, Jesus said:

> "**My sheep hear My voice, and I know them, and they follow Me. And I give them eternal life, and they shall never perish; neither shall anyone snatch them out of My hand.**" (John 10:27-28)

The word **"never"** in this promise is so strongly stated that in the Greek, it took five words to say it. This one English word is a translation of the Greek words **ou me** and **eis ton aiona**, which literally translate as **absolutely not - for ever**. (In the Greek, the word translated **perish** is between these two clauses.) That is, the Greek text literally says **absolutely not perish for ever**.

And here, we also need to consider our Lord's statement, "**neither shall anyone snatch them out of My hand,**" along with His following statement that "**My Father, who has given *them* to Me, is greater than all; and no one is able to snatch *them* out of My Father's hand.**" (John 10:29) And we need to consider these statements in the light of another of His statements, that:

"believes" in this verse again shows that in this case it means something that is in the process of happening, not something that must keep on happening.

This is indicated in a different way by the words "should not perish" in John 3:15 and 16. In both verses, these words are translated from the Greek words **me apoletai**. **Me** is a Greek word meaning not (word number 3361 in Strong's Greek Dictionary.) And **apoletai** is a second aorist subjunctive form of the Greek word **apollymi**, word number 622 in Strong's Greek Dictionary. When an aorist is used in any form other than indicative or participle, there is no time frame involved. It is only a statement of action, with no implication that the action is either continued or completed. So the context of the word "believes" in each of these cases is again definitely not something that must keep on happening.

So we see that in each of the four verses we have examined, although the form of the word "believes" that is used can indeed in some cases mean "keeps on believing," The context in each of these cases makes it plain that it simply means "is believing," and does not even imply a need to "keep on believing." This in not intended to even imply that there is no need to keep on believing. This will be treated in its proper place. Here, the point is only that no such thought is implied in any of these scriptures.

> "This is the will of the Father who sent Me, that of all He has given Me I should lose nothing, but should raise it up at the last day." (John 6:39)

And in the light of the statement by Paul that:

> "I know whom I have believed and am persuaded that He is able to keep what I have committed to Him until that Day." (2 Timothy 1:12b)

And the wonderful closing of Jude 1:

> "Now to Him who is able to keep you from stumbling, And to present *you* faultless Before the presence of His glory with exceeding joy, To God our Savior, Who alone is wise, *Be* glory and majesty, Dominion and power, Both now and forever. Amen." (Jude 1:24-25)

What we need to notice in each of these passages, is that the holding, the keeping, is not accomplished by any imagined power of mere weak believers, but is accomplished by the irresistible power of the almighty God who cannot be defeated.

In examining this all important doctrine, we need to consider Abraham. We read in Hebrews 6:13-14:

> "For when God made a promise to Abraham, because He could swear by no one greater, He swore by Himself, saying, 'Surely blessing I will bless you, and multiplying I will multiply you.'"

This unconditional promise was made to Abraham in Genesis 22:17. But it was more than just a promise. For we are told that God "**confirmed *it* by an oath.**" Why did He do this?

> "For men indeed swear by the greater, and an oath for confirmation *is* for them an end of all dispute. Thus God, determining to show more abundantly to the heirs of promise the immutability of His counsel, confirmed *it* by an oath, that by two immutable things, in which it *is* impossible for God to lie, we might have strong consolation, who have fled for refuge to lay hold of the hope set before *us*." (Hebrews 6:16-18)

God's counsel is immutable. It cannot be changed. When He has made a promise, that promise will most certainly be kept. He wants us to understand this. So He showed it through His promise to Abraham. But He was not satisfied with simply showing it. He wanted to show it **"more abundantly."** So He used man's custom of confirming the promise by an oath. Men swear by something greater than themselves. But there is nothing greater than God. So He swore by Himself. Why did He do this? **"That by two immutable things, in which it *is* impossible for God to lie, we might have strong consolation."**

But how did **"we"** get into the picture. The promise, and the oath, made to Abraham, was made so that **"we might have strong consolation."** Who is the **"we"** here? It is those of us **"who have fled for refuge to lay hold of the hope set before *us*."** And **"This *hope* we have as an anchor of the soul, both sure and steadfast"** and it **"enters the *Presence* behind the veil, where the forerunner has entered for us."** (Hebrews 6:18-19)

Thus we see that this promise and oath, made to Abraham, was not for his sake alone. It was also to teach us a lesson. And what was the lesson? God will most assuredly keep His word. What He has promised He will certainly perform. But why does God make such a strong point of this? We learn this in Galatians 3:15-20:

> "Brethren, I speak in the manner of men: Though *it is* only a man's covenant, yet *if it is* confirmed, no one annuls or adds to it. Now to Abraham and his Seed were the promises made. He does not say, 'And to seeds,' as of

> many, but as of one, *'And to your Seed,'* who is Christ. And this I say, *that* the law, which was four hundred and thirty years later, cannot annul the covenant that was confirmed before by God in Christ, that it should make the promise of no effect. For if the inheritance *is* of the law, *it is* no longer of promise; but God gave *it* to Abraham by promise."

Here we see that the promise was stronger than the law. The Law could not annul the covenant, because that had already been made. But the covenant was not based on law. It was based on promise. Now promise and law are two very different concepts. Law is conditional, as in "If so-and-so, then such-and such." But promise is unconditional, as in "I will do so-and-so." In Galatians 3:15-20, as in Hebrews 6:13-19, our God stressed that His promises are unconditional.

We see this again in a promise made to David, and stressed by repeating it twice in scripture. So we first read:

> "When your days are fulfilled and you rest with your fathers, I will set up your seed after you, who will come from your body, and I will establish his kingdom. He shall build a house for My name, and I will establish the throne of his kingdom forever. I will be his Father, and he shall be My son. If he commits iniquity, I will chasten him with the rod of men and with the blows of the sons of men. But My mercy shall not depart from him, as I took it from Saul, whom I removed from before you. And your house and your kingdom shall be established forever before you. Your throne shall be established forever." (2 Samuel 7:12-16)

And then we also read concerning David:

> "My mercy I will keep for him forever,
> And My covenant shall stand firm with him.
> His seed also I will make *to endure* forever,

> And his throne as the days of heaven.
> 'If his sons forsake My law
> And do not walk in My judgments,
> If they break My statutes
> And do not keep My commandments,
> Then I will punish their transgression with the rod,
> And their iniquity with stripes.
> Nevertheless My lovingkindness I will not utterly take from him,
> Nor allow My faithfulness to fail.
> My covenant I will not break,
> Nor alter the word that has gone out of My lips." (Psalm 89:28-34)

These two remarkable passages describe a promise made to David, and both of them expressly say that absolutely nothing will ever annul it. This promise is remarkable in that both of these two scriptures explicitly state that it cannot even be cancelled by sin.

In 2 Samuel 7, the wording is:

> "If he commits iniquity, I will chasten him with the rod of men and with the blows of the sons of men. But My mercy shall not depart from him, as I took it from Saul, whom I removed from before you."

And in Psalm 89 the wording is:

> "If his sons forsake My law
> And do not walk in My judgments,
> If they break My statutes
> And do not keep My commandments,
> Then I will punish their transgression with the rod,
> And their iniquity with stripes.
> Nevertheless My lovingkindness I will not utterly take from him,
> Nor allow My faithfulness to fail."

In both of these passages God expressly says that sin, if it comes, will be dealt with. But the punishment will not be a cancellation of the promise.

Then, in Psalm 89, God explains this by saying,

> **"My covenant I will not break,**
> **Nor alter the word that has gone out of My lips."**

But what does this mean for us? In Isaiah 55:1-3 we read:

> **"Ho! Everyone who thirsts,**
> **Come to the waters;**
> **And you who have no money,**
> **Come, buy and eat.**
> **Yes, come, buy wine and milk**
> **Without money and without price.**
> **Why do you spend money for** *what is* **not bread,**
> **And your wages for** *what* **does not satisfy?**
> **Listen carefully to Me, and eat** *what is* **good,**
> **And let your soul delight itself in abundance.**
> **Incline your ear, and come to Me.**
> **Hear, and your soul shall live;**
> **And I will make an everlasting covenant with you—**
> **The sure mercies of David."**

So **"the sure mercies of David,"** the absolutely unconditional promise made to David, which can never be annulled, **even by sin**, is here extended to whoever will come, whoever will hear.

Our God made absolutely unconditional promises to Abraham and to David. And He has taught us to apply the unconditional nature of these promises to ourselves. This is not a theory. It is not a conclusion drawn by logic from various passages of scripture. It is expressly stated in the Holy Scriptures. But why does God make such a point of applying these promises to ourselves? Because He has also made similar unconditional promises to us. These promises tell us that He will both save us and keep us. And Romans 11:29 explicitly says that **"the gifts and the calling of God are irrevocable."**

All of this is why eternal security is such a fundamental Christian doctrine. Because our security does not rest upon ourselves, or on anything we do, but upon the irrevocable promise of God, and upon the Lord Jesus Christ, the sacrifice He made at Calvary. That is a firm foundation, which cannot be shaken. In comparison, all else is nothing but shifting sand.

CHAPTER 17

But What About Sin In Our Lives?

The first thing we need to know about sin in the life of a Christian, is that it is totally unacceptable. The question may arise about how much sin can be tolerated in our lives. And the answer is zero. No sin is acceptable. Not any sin of any kind. Not even "a little sin."

> "For if we sin willfully after we have received the knowledge of the truth, there no longer remains a sacrifice for sins, but a certain fearful expectation of judgment, and fiery indignation which will devour the adversaries." (Hebrews 10:26-27)

This is a reference to the law of Moses, in which there were sacrifices for sins committed in ignorance. That is, for things people had done, without knowing that they were forbidden. But there was no sacrifice for a willful sin. Anyone who had knowingly broken one of the commandments could only fearfully wait for punishment. For our God has said that

> "He by no means clears the guilty, visiting the iniquity of the fathers on the children to the third and fourth generation." (Numbers 14:18)

If that were the end of the story, we would all just have to hang our heads, and creep away in fear and shame.

> **"For we all stumble in many things."** (James 3:2)

And:

> **"If we say that we have no sin, we deceive ourselves, and the truth is not in us."** (1 John 1:8)

But this passage goes on say that:

> **"If we confess our sins, He is faithful and just to forgive us our sins and to cleanse us from all unrighteousness"** (1 John 1:9-10)

And then it says:

> **"My little children, these things I write to you, so that you may not sin. And if anyone sins, we have an Advocate with the Father, Jesus Christ the righteous."** (1 John 2:1)

And in another place we read:

> **"For we do not have a High Priest who cannot sympathize with our weaknesses, but was in all *points* tempted as we are, *yet* without sin. Let us therefore come boldly to the throne of grace, that we may obtain mercy and find grace to help in time of need."** (Hebrews 4:15-16)

How it is that we can find forgiveness, when there was no sacrifice for a willful sin? It is because:

> **"the blood of Jesus Christ His Son cleanses us from all sin."** (1 John 1:7)

This is explained in the tenth chapter of Hebrews where, speaking of Jesus, it says:

> "**But this Man, after He had offered one sacrifice for sins forever, sat down at the right hand of God, from that time waiting till His enemies are made His footstool. For by one offering He has perfected forever those who are being sanctified.**" (Hebrews 10:12-14)

And it goes on to say:

> "**Therefore, brethren, having boldness to enter the Holiest by the blood of Jesus, by a new and living way which He consecrated for us, through the veil, that is, His flesh, and *having* a High Priest over the house of God, let us draw near with a true heart in full assurance of faith, having our hearts sprinkled from an evil conscience and our bodies washed with pure water.**" (Hebrews 10:19-22)

This is because:

> "**we have been delivered from the law, having died to what we were held by, so that we should serve in the newness of the Spirit and not *in* the oldness of the letter.**" (Romans 7:6)

And:

> "***There is* therefore now no condemnation to those who are in Christ Jesus, who do not walk according to the flesh, but according to the Spirit. For the law of the Spirit of life in Christ Jesus has made me free from the law of sin and death.**" (Romans 8:1-2)

But that is not all God has to say about this. He also says:

> **"What shall we say then? Shall we continue in sin that grace may abound? Certainly not! How shall we who died to sin live any longer in it?"** (Romans 6:1-2)

And:

> **"Therefore do not let sin reign in your mortal body, that you should obey it in its lusts. And do not present your members *as* instruments of unrighteousness to sin, but present yourselves to God as being alive from the dead, and your members *as* instruments of righteousness to God."** (Romans 6:12-13)

The problem is, how do we do this? If, as we have seen, **"we all stumble in many things,"** and **"If we say that we have no sin, we deceive ourselves,"** then how do we keep sin from reigning in our mortal bodies? The Holy Spirit tells us how to do this. For he said:

> **"The sting of death is sin, and the strength of sin is the law."** (1 Corinthians 15:56)

But He also said that:

> **"the law entered that the offense might abound. But where sin abounded, grace abounded much more, so that as sin reigned in death, even so grace might reign through righteousness to eternal life through Jesus Christ our Lord."** (Romans 5:20-21) For **"Christ has redeemed us from the curse of the law, having become a curse for us (for it is written, 'Cursed is everyone who hangs on a tree')."** (Galatians 3:13)

So we see that **"the strength of sin is the law,"** and that both **"the sting of death is sin"** and **"sin reigned in death."** But **"Christ has redeemed us from the curse of the law."**

> For **"our old man was crucified with *Him*, that the body of sin might be done away with, that we should no longer be slaves of sin. For he who has died has been freed from sin."** (Romans 6:6-7)

"Our old man was crucified with *Him*." Why? **"That we should no longer be slaves of sin."**

> For **"if we died with Christ, we believe that we shall also live with Him, knowing that Christ, having been raised from the dead, dies no more. Death no longer has dominion over Him."** (Romans 6:8-9)

So our instruction is :

> **"Likewise you also, reckon yourselves to be dead indeed to sin, but alive to God in Christ Jesus our Lord."** (Romans 6:11)

For many years, I did not understand the context of this verse. I read it again and again, and said, "but I am **not** dead to sin." For I was interpreting it to mean "dead to the power of sin **to tempt** me." But when we study this passage in its context, we see that this is not what it teaches. Instead, it teaches that we should reckon ourselves dead to the power of sin **to condemn** us. And that is why it says:

> **"For sin shall not have dominion over you, for you are not under law but under grace."** (Romans 6:14)

It does not say "sin **should not** have dominion over you," but **"sin shall not have dominion over you."** That is because the power of sin in our lives is broken, **"for you are not under law but under grace."** And we are truly dead to sin, because having died with Christ, death no longer has power over us. So the power of death, which is the strength of sin, is forever broken in the lives of all who have trusted in Jesus.

Many imagine that this doctrine, like its close associate, eternal security, will only make people assume they can just "get saved," and then do whatever they want to do, sin continually, and not be punished. So they reject both of these as evil doctrines. They think they must keep striving, keep on trying, to live perfect lives. And many of them imagine that, in doing this, they will eventually attain a state of sinless perfection, that sin will no longer be able to tempt them. But the scriptures teach no such idea. Instead, as we have seen they say that:

> **"we all stumble in many things."** (James 3:2)

And:

> **"If we say that we have no sin, we deceive ourselves, and the truth is not in us."** (1 John 1:8)

Being human, we will sin. We will stumble. We will fail. This is not acceptable. But it is a fact of life. The question is not whether or not we will ever manage to put an end to this. (For that will **never** happen.) But what should we do when it does happen? As we have seen, we are specifically told that:

> **"If we confess our sins, He is faithful and just to forgive us our sins and to cleanse us from all unrighteousness."** (1 John 1:9)

We need to notice that this does not even say to ask to be forgiven. It simply says to **"confess our sins."** And when we do, He will **"forgive us our sins."** And He is **"faithful and just"** in doing this, because:

> **"Himself bore our sins in His own body on the tree, that we, having died to sins, might live for righteousness."** (1 Peter 2:24)

The only way we can ever attain real spiritual power in our lives, is to give up the notion that we need to continually strive for sinless perfection. Instead we need to simply rejoice in the fact that:

> **"He has made us accepted in the Beloved."** (Ephesians 1:6)

And so, **"forgetting those things which are behind,"** our past sins, as well as our past triumphs, **"and reaching forward to those things which are ahead,"** we **"press toward the goal for the prize of the upward call of God in Christ Jesus."** (Philippians 3:13-14)

The scriptures teach that **"the joy of the LORD is your strength."** (Nehemiah 8:10) And where does this joy come from? From the fact that **"He has made us accepted in the Beloved."**

> **"For you did not receive the spirit of bondage again to fear, but you received the Spirit of adoption by whom we cry out, 'Abba, Father.' The Spirit Himself bears witness with our spirit that we are children of God, and if children, then heirs--heirs of God and joint heirs with Christ."** (Romans 8:15-17)

This is where our strength lies. And this is the only way we can ever conquer sin in our lives. That is, not by striving for perfection, but by confessing our sin when it happens, and going on our way rejoicing in the fact that we are **"accepted in the beloved."** This **"joy of the Lord"** is the only thing that will ever give us the strength to resist sin in our lives.

CHAPTER 18

The Danger of Falling Away

There are a number of subjects in the Bible for which there is a whole set of passages that clearly teach one idea, and another set of passages that just as clearly teach a second idea which seems to directly contradict the first idea. But whenever that happens, there is always a third set of scriptures that shows how both of these seemingly contradictory ideas can be completely true. One is not true most of the time, and the other exceptions to that general rule. Both are always completely true. And that is the case in the subject now before us.

In the chapters titled "Eternal Security" and "What About Sin In Our Lives," we studied scriptures that explicitly promise that not even sin can make us lose our salvation. But the Bible just as plainly states that those who fall away will most certainly be lost.

> "**For *it is* impossible for those who were once enlightened, and have tasted the heavenly gift, and have become partakers of the Holy Spirit, and have tasted the good word of God and the powers of the age to come, if they fall away, to renew them again to repentance, since they crucify again for themselves the Son of God, and put *Him* to an open shame.**" (Hebrews 6:4-6)

In short, the Bible clearly teaches that those who believe in Jesus are just as certain of heaven as if they were already there, and it just as clearly teaches that those who fall away are just as certain of hell as if they were already there. This indeed **sounds** like a contradiction. But it is not, as we will see in this chapter. For there is a kind of belief that is nothing more than a mental agreement to a fact. We all believe that two plus two is four. But a belief like this is useless in spiritual maters. That is why the scriptures so often use the word **"faith"** instead of the word **"belief."** In fact the NKJV, which we are using, contains the word **"believer"** only once and the words **"having faith"** or **"faithful"** 86 times.

The explanation of the apparent contradiction in the scriptures about salvation begins in the book of James, where we read,"**You believe that there is one God. You do well. Even the demons believe--and tremble!**" (James 2:19) This is pointing out the uselessness of a belief that is nothing but a mental agreement to a fact. "**Even the demons believe**" the facts about God. But demons have no faith. Rather than being servants of God, they are rebels who have chosen to be His enemies. We see this in the case of Judas. Long before Judas openly fell, Jesus said of him, "**Did I not choose you, the twelve, and one of you is a devil?**" (John 6:70) And we see it again in the case of Simon the sorcerer. We read, "**Then Simon himself also believed; and when he was baptized he continued with Philip, and was amazed, seeing the miracles and signs which were done.**" (Acts 8:13) But after he tried to purchase "**the gift of God**" "**with money,**" (Acts 8:20) Peter, in speaking through the Holy Ghost, told him, "**You have neither part nor portion in this matter, for your heart is not right in the sight of God.**" (Acts 8:21) In neither case was it said that the one who fell lost his salvation, but rather that he did not have it. In both cases, their belief was nothing but mental agreement to facts that had been made so obvious as to be undeniable.

But, returning now to Hebrews 6, after the part we already examined, it explains about evil people, saying:

> "**For the earth which drinks in the rain that often comes upon it, and bears herbs useful for those by whom it is cultivated, receives blessing from God; but if it bears thorns and briars, *it is* rejected and near to being cursed, whose end *is* to be burned.**" (Hebrews 6:7-8)

So the test is the fruit. Faith produces fruit. But mere mental agreement to facts produces nothing but thorns and briers.

The Holy Spirit continues:

> **"But, beloved, we are confident of better things concerning you, yes, things that accompany salvation, though we speak in this manner."** (Hebrews 6:9)

In saying this, He was obviously saying that what He had described in verses 4-8 did not accompany salvation. And then He added:

> **"For God *is* not unjust to forget your work and labor of love which you have shown toward His name, *in that* you have ministered to the saints, and do minister."** (Hebrews 6:10)

In saying this, God was saying that it would be unjust for Him to forget all that they had done for Him. That is, that It would be unjust for Him to cancel their salvation.

And if we go back and carefully read the description of the spiritual experiences of those that fall away, we see that it talks all the way around faith, but never actually states that they ever had it. It describes them as **"those who were once enlightened, and have tasted the heavenly gift, and have become partakers of the Holy Spirit, and have tasted the good word of God and the powers of the age to come."** Even at the last supper, when Jesus said, **"Assuredly, I say to you, one of you who eats with Me will betray Me,"** (Mark 14:18) not a single one of the disciples said, "Is it Judas?" Instead, **"they began to be sorrowful, and to say to Him one by one, 'Is it I?' And another *said*, 'Is it I?'"** (Mark 14:19) Judas was **"a devil."** He was not a true believer. But he had gone undetected among them for three years. Not a single one of the twelve even suspected him. In like manner, the people in Hebrews 6 who **"fall away"** are described as experiencing it all, and partaking in all of it, but are not said to have ever had real faith.

Why is this detail important? Because, as we noticed in the chapter on eternal security, the Holy Spirit said through Jude:

> "Now to Him who is able to keep you from stumbling,
> And to present *you* faultless
> Before the presence of His glory with exceeding joy,
> To God our Savior,
> Who alone is wise,
> *Be* glory and majesty,
> Dominion and power,
> Both now and forever.
> Amen." (Jude 1:24-25)

And Jesus said about His sheep, that **"neither shall anyone snatch them out of My hand,"** and that **"no one is able to snatch *them* out of My Father's hand."** (John 10:28-29) These passages clearly say that the Lord Himself will keep those who have truly trusted in Him.

But we are also very clearly told, concerning those that have fallen away, that:

> "They went out from us, but they were not of us; for if they had been of us, they would have continued with us; but *they went out* that they might be made manifest, that none of them were of us." (1 John 2:19)

So the scriptures explain the apparent contradiction between these passages about salvation by telling us two things: First, that God Himself will keep those who are real from falling away, and that those who do fall away thereby prove that the were never real believers. They only had a mental agreement to the facts of salvation, but did not have faith in the Savior.

So what should we do if we find ourselves tempted to fall away? We are instructed to:

> "Examine yourselves *as to* whether you are in the faith. Test yourselves. Do you not know yourselves, that Jesus Christ is in you?--unless indeed you are disqualified." (2 Corinthians 13:5)

But how do we **"examine"** ourselves? How do we **"test"** ourselves? The Holy Spirit has given us a test, saying:

> "Now the works of the flesh are evident, which are: adultery, fornication, uncleanness, lewdness, idolatry, sorcery, hatred, contentions, jealousies, outbursts of wrath, selfish ambitions, dissensions, heresies, envy, murders, drunkenness, revelries, and the like; of which I tell you beforehand, just as I also told *you* in time past, that those who practice such things will not inherit the kingdom of God." (Galatians 5:19-21)
>
> "But the fruit of the Spirit is love, joy, peace, longsuffering, kindness, goodness, faithfulness, gentleness, self-control. Against such there is no law." (Galatians 5:22-23)

So if you find yourself tempted to fall away, examine these two lists. Which one more accurately describes you? Almost no one will completely match either list. Very few modern people will find themselves guilty of **"idolatry"** or **"murders."** But how about **"hatred, contentions, jealousies, outbursts of wrath, selfish ambitions,"** and **"dissensions"**? Or, perish the thought, **"adultery, fornication, uncleanness,"** or **"lewdness."** Or are you characterized by **"love, joy, peace, longsuffering, kindness, goodness, faithfulness, gentleness,"** and **"self-control"**?

Which list is more like yourself? If you are closer to the first list than to the second one, you need to get right with God. But how do you do that? It is not by "turning over a new leaf," nor is it a matter of trying harder. Instead, you need to fall on your knees and, like the tax collector Jesus told about, cry out, **"God, be merciful to me a sinner!"** (Luke 18:13) When this is done in faith, His promise is **"the one who comes to Me I will by no means cast out."** (John 6:37)

But remember, the instruction is not just to **"believe in the gospel,"** but to **"Repent, and believe in the gospel."** (Mark 1:15) For **"God… commands all men everywhere to repent."** (Acts 17:30)

And:

> **"without faith *it is* impossible to please *Him*, for he who comes to God must believe that He is, and *that* He is a rewarder of those who diligently seek Him."** (Hebrews 11:6)

CHAPTER 19

The Coming of Christ for His Own

The basic scripture about our Lord's coming for His own is:

> "But I do not want you to be ignorant, brethren, concerning those who have fallen asleep, lest you sorrow as others who have no hope. For if we believe that Jesus died and rose again, even so God will bring with Him those who sleep in Jesus. For this we say to you by the word of the Lord, that we who are alive *and* remain until the coming of the Lord will by no means precede those who are asleep. For the Lord Himself will descend from heaven with a shout, with the voice of an archangel, and with the trumpet of God. And the dead in Christ will rise first. Then we who are alive *and* remain shall be caught up together with them in the clouds to meet the Lord in the air. And thus we shall always be with the Lord. Therefore comfort one another with these words." (1 Thessalonians 4:13-18)

This scripture is basically intended as comfort for those of us who have lost loved ones who had trusted in Christ, but it also, and very clearly, states that our Lord will indeed come back and take all of us who have trusted in Himself, to be forever with Him. But where will that be? Jesus Himself said:

> "Let not your heart be troubled; you believe in God, believe also in Me. In My Father's house are many mansions; if *it were* not so, I would have told you. I go to prepare a place for you. And if I go and prepare a place for you, I will come again and receive you to Myself; that where I am, *there* you may be also." (John 14:1-3)

So the place that is prepared for us is in His **"Father's house,"** that is, in heaven. And that is where He has promised to take us.

The Thessalonians were commended in that they had

> **"turned to God from idols to serve the living and true God, and to wait for His Son from heaven."** (1 Thessalonians 1:9-10)

And Christians are instructed to be eager in this waiting. For Philippians 3:20-21 says:

> **"For our citizenship is in heaven, from which we also eagerly wait for the Savior, the Lord Jesus Christ, who will transform our lowly body that it may be conformed to His glorious body, according to the working by which He is able even to subdue all things to Himself."**

And Hebrews 9:27-28 says:

> **"And as it is appointed for men to die once, but after this the judgment, so Christ was offered once to bear the sins of many. To those who eagerly wait for Him He will appear a second time, apart from sin, for salvation."** Again, Galatians 5:5 says, **"For we through the Spirit eagerly wait for the hope of righteousness by faith."**

And 1 Corinthians 1:7 says:

> "you come short in no gift, eagerly waiting for the revelation of our Lord Jesus Christ."

Again, we read:

> "For we know that the whole creation groans and labors with birth pangs together until now. Not only *that*, but we also who have the firstfruits of the Spirit, even we ourselves groan within ourselves, eagerly waiting for the adoption, the redemption of our body. For we were saved in this hope, but hope that is seen is not hope; for why does one still hope for what he sees? But if we hope for what we do not see, we eagerly wait for *it* with perseverance." (Romans 8:22-25)

We need to notice the Greek word translated **eagerly wait for** or **eagerly waiting for** in each of these passages, and twice in the last one. It is **apekdechomai.** (word number 556 in Strong's Greek Dictionary.) It does not just mean to **wait for**, as it is rendered in some translations, but to **expectfully wait for.** So we see that our translation is indeed correct in including the word **eagerly** in each of these places. For the Greek text does not just convey the thought of **waiting for** His coming, but of **eagerly waiting for** it.

And why should we be so eager in this waiting? There are two reasons. The first is that the scriptures call this our **"blessed hope,"** saying:

> "looking for the blessed hope and glorious appearing of our great God and Savior Jesus Christ," (Titus 2:13)

And promise "the crown of righteousness" to "all who have loved" this "appearing," saying:

> "Finally, there is laid up for me the crown of righteousness, which the Lord, the righteous Judge, will give to me on

> that Day, and not to me only but also to all who have loved His appearing." (2 Timothy 4:8)

But there is a second reason why we should be eager in this waiting. Jesus said:

> "But of that day and hour no one knows, not even the angels in heaven, nor the Son, but only the Father. Take heed, watch and pray; for you do not know when the time is. *It is* like a man going to a far country, who left his house and gave authority to his servants, and to each his work, and commanded the doorkeeper to watch. Watch therefore, for you do not know when the master of the house is coming--in the evening, at midnight, at the crowing of the rooster, or in the morning-- lest, coming suddenly, he find you sleeping. And what I say to you, I say to all: Watch!" (Mark 13:32-37)

While the scriptures tell us many things that must happen before Christ comes to judge the wicked and deliver Israel, they tell us nothing that must happen before He comes for His own. This is always presented in the scriptures as a present hope, something that might take place at any time.

We see this repeatedly in the book of Revelation, where we read:

> "Behold, I am coming quickly! Hold fast what you have, that no one may take your crown." (Revelation 3:11)
> "Behold, I am coming quickly! Blessed *is* he who keeps the words of the prophecy of this book." (Revelation 22:7)
> "He who testifies to these things says, 'Surely I am coming quickly.' Amen. Even so, come, Lord Jesus!" (Revelation 22:20)
> "And behold, I am coming quickly, and My reward *is* with Me, to give to every one according to his work." (Revelation 22:12)

The Greek word translated **quickly** in each of these places is **tachu**. (word number 5035 in Strong's Greek Dictionary) It means **shortly**, that is, **without delay, soon,** or **suddenly**. So **quickly** is indeed an accurate translation of this Greek word, as used in these sentences. But it also can legitimately be translated as "suddenly," that is, without any warning of any kind.

So the scriptures indeed tell us, and very clearly tell us, that our Lord is coming to take us to His Father's house, that is, to heaven. And they both call this our **"blessed hope"** and teach us to **"eagerly"** await this blessed and wonderful event. Because it is something to be expected at any time, without warning.

CHAPTER 20

The Coming of Christ to Judge the Wicked

This great event was prophesied even before the great flood which took place in the days of Noah.

> "Now Enoch, the seventh from Adam, prophesied about these men also, saying, 'Behold, the Lord comes with ten thousands of His saints, to execute judgment on all, to convict all who are ungodly among them of all their ungodly deeds which they have committed in an ungodly way, and of all the harsh things which ungodly sinners have spoken against Him.'" (Jude 1:14-15)

The Holy Spirit said through Peter that:

> "scoffers will come in the last days, walking according to their own lusts, and saying, 'Where is the promise of His coming? For since the fathers fell asleep, all things continue as they were from the beginning of creation.'" (2 Peter 3:3-4)

But the fact that men scoff changes nothing. For He will indeed come, just as he said.

This coming is symbolically described in Revelation 19:11-16:

> "Now I saw heaven opened, and behold, a white horse. And He who sat on him was called Faithful and True, and in righteousness He judges and makes war. His eyes *were* like a flame of fire, and on His head *were* many crowns. He had a name written that no one knew except Himself. He *was* clothed with a robe dipped in blood, and His name is called The Word of God. And the armies in heaven, clothed in fine linen, white and clean, followed Him on white horses. Now out of His mouth goes a sharp sword, that with it He should strike the nations. And He Himself will rule them with a rod of iron. He Himself treads the winepress of the fierceness and wrath of Almighty God. And He has on *His* robe and on His thigh a name written:
>
> KING OF KINGS
> AND LORD OF LORDS."

While the language here is clearly symbolic, its meaning is obviously that the Lord will come in an awesome display of power and glory. Beside this, the "shock and awe" of recent military attacks pales into nothingness. But a factual statement of His coming, as opposed to this symbolic vision, is:

> "behold, the LORD will come with fire And with His chariots, like a whirlwind, To render His anger with fury, And His rebuke with flames of fire. For by fire and by His sword The LORD will judge all flesh; And the slain of the LORD shall be many." (Isaiah 66:15-16)

Again, we read that:

> "'A noise will come to the ends of the earth-- For the LORD has a controversy with the nations; He will plead His case with all flesh. He will give those who are wicked to the sword,' says the LORD." (Jeremiah 25:31)

So we read:

> "Enter into the rock, and hide in the dust,
> From the terror of the LORD
> And the glory of His majesty.
> The lofty looks of man shall be humbled,
> The haughtiness of men shall be bowed down,
> And the LORD alone shall be exalted in that day.
> For the day of the LORD of hosts
> *Shall come* upon everything proud and lofty,
> Upon everything lifted up--
> And it shall be brought low–" (Isaiah 2:10-12)

And:

> "Behold, the LORD makes the earth empty and makes it waste,
> Distorts its surface
> And scatters abroad its inhabitants.
> And it shall be:
> As with the people, so with the priest;
> As with the servant, so with his master;
> As with the maid, so with her mistress;
> As with the buyer, so with the seller;
> As with the lender, so with the borrower;
> As with the creditor, so with the debtor." (Isaiah 24:1-2)

And:

> "behold, the LORD is coming out of His place;
> He will come down
> And tread on the high places of the earth.
> The mountains will melt under Him,
> And the valleys will split
> Like wax before the fire,
> Like waters poured down a steep place." (Micah 1:3-4)
> "And in that day His feet will stand on the Mount of Olives, Which faces Jerusalem on the east. And the Mount of Olives shall be split in two, From east to west, *Making* a very large valley; Half of the mountain shall move toward the north And half of it toward the south. Then you shall flee *through* My mountain valley, For the mountain valley shall reach to Azal. Yes, you shall flee As you fled from the earthquake In the days of Uzziah king of Judah. Thus the LORD my God will come, *And* all the saints with You." (Zechariah 14:4-5)

And of yet another symbolic vision, we read:

> "God came from Teman,
> The Holy One from Mount Paran.
> Selah
> His glory covered the heavens,
> And the earth was full of His praise.
> His brightness was like the light;
> He had rays *flashing* from His hand,
> And there His power *was* hidden.
> Before Him went pestilence,
> And fever followed at His feet.
> He stood and measured the earth;
> He looked and startled the nations.
> And the everlasting mountains were scattered,
> The perpetual hills bowed.

> His ways *are* everlasting.
> I saw the tents of Cushan in affliction;
> The curtains of the land of Midian trembled.
> O LORD, were *You* displeased with the rivers,
> *Was* Your anger against the rivers,
> *Was* Your wrath against the sea,
> That You rode on Your horses,
> Your chariots of salvation?
> Your bow was made quite ready;
> Oaths were sworn over *Your* arrows.
> Selah
> You divided the earth with rivers.
> The mountains saw You *and* trembled;
> The overflowing of the water passed by.
> The deep uttered its voice,
> *And* lifted its hands on high.
> The sun and moon stood still in their habitation;
> At the light of Your arrows they went,
> At the shining of Your glittering spear.
> You marched through the land in indignation;
> You trampled the nations in anger." (Habakkuk 3:3-12)

We have examined so many of these scriptures to clearly see that this is indeed presented in the Bible, and insisted upon in many places, as an actual future event that will be terrible beyond comprehension.

So we will close this study by going back and noticing the conclusion of the passage in 2 Peter 3 about the **"scoffers"** that **"will come in the last days."** the Holy Spirit went on to say:

> "But, beloved, do not forget this one thing, that with the Lord one day is as a thousand years, and a thousand years as one day. The Lord is not slack concerning *His* promise, as some count slackness, but is longsuffering toward us, not willing that any should perish but that all should come to repentance. But the day of the Lord will come as a thief in the night, in which the heavens

> will pass away with a great noise, and the elements will melt with fervent heat; both the earth and the works that are in it will be burned up. Therefore, since all these things will be dissolved, what manner *of persons* ought you to be in holy conduct and godliness, looking for and hastening the coming of the day of God, because of which the heavens will be dissolved, being on fire, and the elements will melt with fervent heat? Nevertheless we, according to His promise, look for new heavens and a new earth in which righteousness dwells." (2 Peter 3:8-13)

So we see that the scriptures do indeed state, and very clearly and repeatedly state, that there is a day coming, when the God of heaven will come to judge the wicked of this world. And they make it absolutely clear that this coming will be terrible beyond description. The only protection from this wrath is to make peace with God while you still can,

> **"while it is said: *'Today, if you will hear His voice, Do not harden your hearts.'"*** (Hebrews 3:15)

For there is a day coming when it will be too late.

CHAPTER 21

The Coming of Christ to Deliver Israel

Some will be shocked at the idea that the coming of Christ to deliver Israel should be presented as a fundamental of the faith. For it is denied by many Christians. And even among those that believe it, most do not consider this doctrine fundamental. But it is fundamental, because it affects the very basic foundations of the Christian faith.

In the chapter titled "The Faithfulness of God," we saw that there is no doctrine more essential to basic and fundamental Christianity, than the faithfulness of God. Our entire hope is built on the reliability of the word of God, on the fact that we can absolutely trust Him to do exactly what He said He would do. If His promises are not absolutely reliable, then we have no basis for our faith. Without this secure foundation, we have nothing. Indeed, the scriptures themselves say that:

> "If in this life only we have hope in Christ, we are of all men the most pitiable." (1 Corinthians 15:19)

Now many, even many real and sincere Christians, think that in the promises of the Old Testament, when God said Israel, He meant "the church." and when He said "the land," He meant heaven. And many argue this idea very convincingly. But it neglects one basic fact. And that fact is that God made these promises to a **particular** people, to a **specific** nation. And if He could faithfully tell **that** nation that He was not really speaking about them, but was actually speaking about a different people that would come in the future, He could just as faithfully tell **us** that the promises He made to **us** were not really meant for **us**, but for a different people that would come in the future. If the promises of God are not absolutely reliable, then our faith is worthless.

These people imagine that the language of Bible prophecy is symbolic, that nothing means what it says, but always means something different. And as long as the subject is only prophetic dreams or visions, this has merit. For without a single exception in the entire Bible, every prophetic dream or vision which is accompanied by an inspired interpretation, had a meaning entirely different from what had been seen. But that is not the case with explicitly stated promises, or with explicit statements that specific things will happen. A case in point here is a long section of Daniel 11, running from verse 2 through verse 35. This section covers a series of wars that lasted about 130 years, and is so precisely accurate, down to the tiniest detail, that unbelievers argue that its very accuracy proves that it could not have been written until after these events had taken place. But we are specifically told that this vision was given to Daniel, long before even the beginning of that 130 year period.

Now many of the people who argue as we have been speaking, are simply ignorant of the way many of these prophecies are stated. They are not aware that many of them are stated in language that cannot even rationally be re-interpreted to mean anything different from what they say. One such case is found in Jeremiah 16:14-15, where we read:

> " 'Therefore behold, the days are coming,' says the LORD, 'that it shall no more be said, "The LORD lives who brought up the children of Israel from the land of Egypt," but, "The LORD lives who brought up the children of Israel from the land of the north and from all the lands where He had driven them." For I will bring them back into their land which I gave to their fathers.' "

"Their land" is defined in Ezekiel 36, where the **"mountains of Israel,"** along with **"the hills, the rivers, the valleys, the desolate wastes, and the cities that have been forsaken,"** (verse 4) are promised that:

> "you shall shoot forth your branches and yield your fruit to My people Israel, for they are about to come. For indeed I am for you, and I will turn to you, and you shall be tilled and sown. I will multiply men upon you, all the house of Israel, all of it; and the cities shall be inhabited and the ruins rebuilt. I will multiply upon you man and beast; and they shall increase and bear young; I will make you inhabited as in former times, and do better for you than at your beginnings. Then you shall know that I am the LORD." (Ezekiel 36:8-11)

And Ezekiel 47:13-20 goes so far as to precisely define the future borders of **"their land,"** saying:

> "Thus says the Lord GOD: 'These *are* the borders by which you shall divide the land as an inheritance among the twelve tribes of Israel. Joseph *shall have two* portions. You shall inherit it equally with one another; for I raised My hand in an oath to give it to your fathers, and this land shall fall to you as your inheritance. This *shall be* the border of the land on the north: from the Great Sea, *by* the road to Hethlon, as one goes to Zedad, Hamath, Berothah, Sibraim (which *is* between the border of Damascus and the border of Hamath), to Hazar Hatticon (which *is* on the border of Hauran). Thus the boundary shall be from the Sea to Hazar Enan, the border of Damascus; and as for the north, northward, it is the border of Hamath. *This is* the north side. On the east side you shall mark out the border from between Hauran and Damascus, and between Gilead and the land of Israel, along the Jordan, and along the eastern side of the sea.

> *This is* the east side. The south side, toward the South, *shall be* from Tamar to the waters of Meribah by Kadesh, along the brook to the Great Sea. *This is* the south side, toward the South. The west side *shall be* the Great Sea, from the *southern* boundary until one comes to a point opposite Hamath. This *is* the west side.' " (Ezekiel 47:13-20)

And the following chapter, Ezekiel 48, defines how **"their land"** is to be divided among the twelve tribes of Israel, saying:

> "Now these *are* the names of the tribes: From the northern border along the road to Hethlon at the entrance of Hamath, to Hazar Enan, the border of Damascus northward, in the direction of Hamath, *there shall be* one *section for* Dan from its east to its west side; by the border of Dan, from the east side to the west, one *section for* Asher; by the border of Asher, from the east side to the west, one *section for* Naphtali; by the border of Naphtali, from the east side to the west, one *section for* Manasseh; by the border of Manasseh, from the east side to the west, one *section for* Ephraim; by the border of Ephraim, from the east side to the west, one *section for* Reuben; by the border of Reuben, from the east side to the west, one *section for* Judah; "by the border of Judah, from the east side to the west, shall be the district which you shall set apart, twenty-five thousand *cubits* in width, and *in* length the same as one of the *other* portions, from the east side to the west, with the sanctuary in the center." (Ezekiel 48:1-8)

And:

> " 'As for the rest of the tribes, from the east side to the west, Benjamin *shall have* one *section;* by the border of Benjamin, from the east side to the west, Simeon *shall*

> *have* one *section;* by the border of Simeon, from the east side to the west, Issachar *shall have* one *section;* by the border of Issachar, from the east side to the west, Zebulun *shall have* one *section;* by the border of Zebulun, from the east side to the west, Gad *shall have* one *section;* by the border of Gad, on the south side, toward the South, the border shall be from Tamar *to* the waters of Meribah *by* Kadesh, along the brook to the Great Sea. This *is* the land which you shall divide by lot as an inheritance among the tribes of Israel, and these *are* their portions,' says the Lord GOD." (Ezekiel 48:23-29)

In Ezekiel 43:13, the cubit being used was defined as **"the cubit is one cubit and a handbreadth."** This was sometimes called the great cubit, and was 22 inches long. So the center section. **"twenty-five thousand cubits in width,"** works out to 8.68 miles wide. Verses 9-22 specify how this section is to be divided.

There is simply no rational way to even try to pretend that all this specific detail does not actually mean what it so plainly says.

Again, the people who desire to interpret these scriptures to mean something different from what they say, imagine that the promises were only made to the children of Abraham, and point out that the scriptures clearly state that those that share the faith of Abraham are the children of Abraham. And if the only promises in question were those made to Abraham, this argument would have at least some merit. But there were not only promises made to Abraham. Other promises were specifically and explicitly made to many of his descendants. We have just noticed a promise made to **"all the house of Israel, all of it."** The Hebrew wording here translated **"all - all of it,"** is the Hebrew word **kol** doubled. This is word number 3605 in Strong's Hebrew Dictionary. In this passage, this Hebrew word which literally translates as the English word **all**, is doubled to stress that the meaning is **absolutely** all of **"the house of Israel."** Again, we read:

> "It shall come to pass in that day That the Lord shall set His hand again the second time To recover the remnant of His people who are left, From Assyria and Egypt, From Pathros and Cush, From Elam and Shinar, From Hamath and the islands of the sea. He will set up a banner for the nations, And will assemble the outcasts of Israel, And gather together the dispersed of Judah From the four corners of the earth. Also the envy of Ephraim shall depart, And the adversaries of Judah shall be cut off; Ephraim shall not envy Judah, And Judah shall not harass Ephraim." (Isaiah 11:11-13)

So now we see an explicitly stated promise, made not only to the ancient nation of Israel, but to the two ancient sub-nations of Judah and Ephraim. And we have already noticed that Ezekiel 48 extends this promise to each of the ancient twelve tribes of Israel by name. While there is some logic in arguing that in some passages of scripture, the name "Israel" at least seems to be equated with "the church," there is absolutely no excuse, anywhere in the entire Bible, for applying this same logic to the names of the sub-nations of Judah and Ephraim, or to the names of any of the twelve tribes of Israel. Nor does any scripture contain any excuse for interpreting the name "Jacob" to mean "the church." Yet we read in Isaiah 41:14:

> "'Fear not, you worm Jacob, You men of Israel! I will help you,' says the LORD And your Redeemer, the Holy One of Israel."

Again, although there is some logic in arguing that "the children of Abraham" means "the church," this logic cannot be used in regard to **"the sons of Zadok."** For we read:

> "'But the priests, the Levites, the sons of Zadok, who kept charge of My sanctuary when the children of Israel went astray from Me, they shall come near Me to minister to Me; and they shall stand before Me to offer to Me the fat

> and the blood,' says the Lord GOD. They shall enter My sanctuary, and they shall come near My table to minister to Me, and they shall keep My charge." (Ezekiel 44:15-16)

Nor can this logic be used in regard to "**the family of the house of David.**" Or to "**the family of the house of Nathan,**" "**the family of the house of Levi,**" or "**the family of the house of Shimei.**" For all of these are explicitly named in regard to the repentant mourning that will take place when Messiah returns.

> "And the land shall mourn, every family by itself: the family of the house of David by itself, and their wives by themselves; the family of the house of Nathan by itself, and their wives by themselves; the family of the house of Levi by itself, and their wives by themselves; the family of Shimei by itself, and their wives by themselves; all the families that remain, every family by itself, and their wives by themselves." (Zechariah 12:11-13)

Nor can this logic be used of "**Phinehas the son of Eleazar,**" of whom we read that the Lord said:

> " 'Phinehas the son of Eleazar, the son of Aaron the priest, has turned back My wrath from the children of Israel, because he was zealous with My zeal among them, so that I did not consume the children of Israel in My zeal.' Therefore say, 'Behold, I give to him My covenant of peace; and it shall be to him and his descendants after him a covenant of an everlasting priesthood, because he was zealous for his God, and made atonement for the children of Israel.' " (Numbers 25:11-13)

Nor can this logic be used of "**Jonadab the son of Rechab,**" of whom

> "Jeremiah said to the house of the Rechabites, 'Thus says the LORD of hosts, the God of Israel: "Because you have obeyed the commandment of Jonadab your father, and kept all his precepts and done according to all that he commanded you, therefore thus says the LORD of hosts, the God of Israel: 'Jonadab the son of Rechab shall not lack a man to stand before Me forever.' " ' " (Jeremiah 35:18-19)

So we see that there are explicitly stated promises made, not only to the children of Abraham, but to the physical land of Israel, to the nation of Israel, even calling it **"Jacob,"** to the sub-nations of Judah and Ephraim, to each of the twelve tribes of Israel by name, to the families of the houses of David, Nathan. Levi, and Shimei, and to the descendants of Zadok, Phinehas and Jonadab. Thus we see that, aside from simple ignorance of the scriptures, it is nothing short of unbelief to deny that Christ will indeed come to deliver Israel.

Those that want to reduce all this explicitly stated language to symbolism, often claim hat these promises were fulfilled in the return described in the books of Ezra and Nehemiah. But that return involved only a very small part of the sub-kingdom of Judah, not even approximately the **"all the house of Israel, all of it"** promised in Ezekiel 36:10. In defense of that claim, they often point out that the scriptures say that only a remnant of Israel will return, quoting such scriptures as:

> "And it shall come to pass in that day *That* the remnant of Israel, And such as have escaped of the house of Jacob, Will never again depend on him who defeated them, But will depend on the LORD, the Holy One of Israel, in truth. The remnant will return, the remnant of Jacob, To the Mighty God." (Isaiah 10:20-21) And **"Therefore He shall give them up, Until the time *that* she who is in labor has given birth; Then the remnant of His brethren Shall return to the children of Israel."** (Micah 5:3)

This indeed seems to contradict such passages as Ezekiel 36:10, but it does not. For before the time at which these promises will apply, the **"the house of Israel"** will have been severely purged. This is stated in two prophecies.

Concerning those already in the land at the time of the great tribulation, the Lord said:

> " 'And it shall come to pass in all the land,' Says the LORD, '*That* two-thirds in it shall be cut off *and* die, But *one*-third shall be left in it: I will bring the *one*-third through the fire, Will refine them as silver is refined, And test them as gold is tested. They will call on My name, And I will answer them. I will say, "This *is* My people"; And each one will say, "The LORD *is* my God." ' " (Zechariah 13:8-9)

And concerning those that the Lord will bring back to **"their land"** when He returns, He said:

> " '*As* I live,' says the Lord GOD, 'surely with a mighty hand, with an outstretched arm, and with fury poured out, I will rule over you. I will bring you out from the peoples and gather you out of the countries where you are scattered, with a mighty hand, with an outstretched arm, and with fury poured out. And I will bring you into the wilderness of the peoples, and there I will plead My case with you face to face. Just as I pleaded My case with your fathers in the wilderness of the land of Egypt, so I will plead My case with you,' says the Lord GOD. 'I will make you pass under the rod, and I will bring you into the bond of the covenant; I will purge the rebels from among you, and those who transgress against Me; I will bring them out of the country where they dwell, but they shall not enter the land of Israel. Then you will know that I *am* the LORD.' " (Ezekiel 20:33-38)

So after these purges have been completed, **"all the house of Israel, all of it,"** will have been reduced to a mere remnant of what it had been only a short time earlier. And two of the prophecies about the spiritual restoration of Israel explicitly state that this restoration will only apply to the survivors of these purges. First, the Lord said:

> "In that day the Branch of the LORD shall be beautiful and glorious; And the fruit of the earth *shall be* excellent and appealing For those of Israel who have escaped. And it shall come to pass that *he who is* left in Zion and remains in Jerusalem will be called holy--everyone who is recorded among the living in Jerusalem. When the Lord has washed away the filth of the daughters of Zion, and purged the blood of Jerusalem from her midst, by the spirit of judgment and by the spirit of burning." (Isaiah 4:2-4)

And then, as we have already noticed in a different context, He said:

> "And I will pour on the house of David and on the inhabitants of Jerusalem the Spirit of grace and supplication; then they will look on Me whom they pierced. Yes, they will mourn for Him as one mourns for *his* only *son,* and grieve for Him as one grieves for a firstborn. In that day there shall be a great mourning in Jerusalem, like the mourning at Hadad Rimmon in the plain of Megiddo. And the land shall mourn, every family by itself: the family of the house of David by itself, and their wives by themselves; the family of the house of Nathan by itself, and their wives by themselves; the family of the house of Levi by itself, and their wives by themselves; the family of Shimei by itself, and their wives by themselves; all the families that remain, every family by itself, and their wives by themselves." (Zechariah 12:10-14)

So we see that there is no contradiction between the scriptures that say that the restoration will involve **"all the house of Israel, all of it,"** and the scriptures that say **"The remnant will return, the remnant of Jacob, To the Mighty God."** And thus we indeed see that the promised return is indeed a return of absolutely all of the ancient nation of Israel, and has most certainly never been fulfilled.

The coming of Christ to deliver Israel takes place at the same time as His coming to judge the wicked. That is, this coming will have a dual purpose, both to judge the wicked and to deliver Israel.

This becomes clear in the prophecy we previously examined in Zechariah 14, about the great earthquake that will take place when the Lord's feet touch the Mount of Olives. This prophecy goes on to say:

> "And in that day it shall be *That* living waters shall flow from Jerusalem, Half of them toward the eastern sea And half of them toward the western sea; In both summer and winter it shall occur. And the LORD shall be King over all the earth. In that day it shall be-- 'The LORD is one,' And His name one. All the land shall be turned into a plain from Geba to Rimmon south of Jerusalem. *Jerusalem* shall be raised up and inhabited in her place from Benjamin's Gate to the place of the First Gate and the Corner Gate, and *from* the Tower of Hananeel to the king's winepresses. *The people* shall dwell in it; And no longer shall there be utter destruction, But Jerusalem shall be safely inhabited." (Zechariah 14:8-11)

We see this again in the passage we examined from Habakkuk 3 about God coming with **"rays *flashing* from His hand."** For the next verse after the part we already read says:

> "You went forth for the salvation of Your people, For salvation with Your Anointed. You struck the head from the house of the wicked, By laying bare from foundation to neck. Selah" (Habakkuk 3:13)

But this is conclusive in the passage we previously examined in Isaiah 66 about the Lord coming **"with fire," "To render His anger with fury, And His rebuke with flames of fire."** For that passage goes on to say:

> "'For I know their works and their thoughts. It shall be that I will gather all nations and tongues; and they shall come and see My glory. I will set a sign among them; and those among them who escape I will send to the nations: to Tarshish and Pul and Lud, who draw the bow, and Tubal and Javan, to the coastlands afar off who have not heard My fame nor seen My glory. And they shall declare My glory among the Gentiles. Then they shall bring all your brethren for an offering to the LORD out of all nations, on horses and in chariots and in litters, on mules and on camels, to My holy mountain Jerusalem,' says the LORD, 'as the children of Israel bring an offering in a clean vessel into the house of the LORD. And I will also take some of them for priests and Levites,' says the LORD." (Isaiah 66:18-21)

So it is absolutely clear that the Lord will accomplish these two purposes in a single coming. But what about the promises to deliver **"Judah and Jerusalem,"** and **"the remnant of Israel"**? What do the scriptures actually say about these? During the tribulation period Jerusalem will be under siege, as we read:

> "Woe to Ariel, to Ariel, the city *where* David dwelt! add ye year to year; let them kill sacrifices. Yet I will distress Ariel, and there shall be heaviness and sorrow: and it shall be unto me as Ariel. And I will camp against thee round about, and will lay siege against thee with a mount, and I will raise forts against thee." (Isaiah 29:1-3)

But then we read:

> "Moreover the multitude of your foes Shall be like fine dust, And the multitude of the terrible ones Like chaff that passes away; Yes, it shall be in an instant, suddenly. You will be punished by the LORD of hosts With thunder and earthquake and great noise, *With* storm and tempest And the flame of devouring fire. The multitude of all the nations who fight against Ariel, Even all who fight against her and her fortress, And distress her, Shall be as a dream of a night vision." (Isaiah 29:5-7)

The Lord says of that deliverance that:

> "I will remove far from you the northern *army*, And will drive him away into a barren and desolate land, With his face toward the eastern sea And his back toward the western sea; His stench will come up, And his foul odor will rise, Because he has done monstrous things." (Joel 2:20)

And:

> "Therefore thus says the Lord GOD of hosts: 'O My people, who dwell in Zion, do not be afraid of the Assyrian. He shall strike you with a rod and lift up his staff against you, in the manner of Egypt. For yet a very little while and the indignation will cease, as will My anger in their destruction.' And the LORD of hosts will stir up a scourge for him like the slaughter of Midian at the rock of Oreb; as His rod was on the sea, so will He lift it up in the manner of Egypt." (Isaiah 10:24-26)

And again:

> "when I shall bring again the captivity of Judah and Jerusalem, I will also gather all nations, and will bring

> them down into the valley of Jehoshaphat, and will plead with them there *for* my people and for my heritage Israel, whom they have scattered among the nations, and parted my land." (Joel 3:1-2)

In connection with this great deliverance, we read:

> "And it shall come to pass in that day *That* the remnant of Israel, And such as have escaped of the house of Jacob, Will never again depend on him who defeated them, But will depend on the LORD, the Holy One of Israel, in truth. The remnant will return, the remnant of Jacob, To the Mighty God. For though your people, O Israel, be as the sand of the sea, A remnant of them will return; The destruction decreed shall overflow with righteousness." (Isaiah 10:20-22)

We have already noticed the bitter weeping of their repentance at that time. The result will be that:

> "In that day you shall not be shamed for any of your deeds In which you transgress against Me; For then I will take away from your midst Those who rejoice in your pride, And you shall no longer be haughty In My holy mountain. I will leave in your midst A meek and humble people, And they shall trust in the name of the LORD. The remnant of Israel shall do no unrighteousness And speak no lies, Nor shall a deceitful tongue be found in their mouth; For they shall feed *their* flocks and lie down, And no one shall make *them* afraid." (Zephaniah 3:11-13)

And:

> "No more shall every man teach his neighbor, and every man his brother, saying, 'Know the LORD,' for they all

> shall know Me, from the least of them to the greatest of them, says the LORD. For I will forgive their iniquity, and their sin I will remember no more." (Jeremiah 31:34)

This, then, is the wonderful deliverance that our Lord Jesus, the great promised Messiah of Israel, will rain down upon His people Israel in a future day. He has promised it. And His word is sure.

This chapter has been so long because there are so very many who do not realize its importance, that it is actually fundamental Christian doctrine. And that is, at least in part, because they have not noticed what even the New Testament says about these promises.

In this respect, we need to notice what the Holy Spirit said about the promise as it was first made to Abraham. He said:

> "For when God made a promise to Abraham, because He could swear by no one greater, He swore by Himself, saying, 'Surely blessing I will bless you, and multiplying I will multiply you.' And so, after he had patiently endured, he obtained the promise. For men indeed swear by the greater, and an oath for confirmation *is* for them an end of all dispute. Thus God, determining to show more abundantly to the heirs of promise the immutability of His counsel, confirmed *it* by an oath, that by two immutable things, in which it *is* impossible for God to lie, we might have strong consolation, who have fled for refuge to lay hold of the hope set before *us*. This *hope* we have as an anchor of the soul, both sure and steadfast, and which enters the Presence *behind* the veil." (Hebrews 6:13-19)

Here we need to notice that the absolute immutability of this promise, as it was made to Abraham, is applied to ourselves. The promise itself was only made to Abraham. But the immutable nature of that promise is applied to us, saying, **"that by two immutable things, in which it *is* impossible for God to lie, we might have strong consolation."** And who are the "we"? We **"who have fled for refuge to lay hold of the hope set before *us*."** And **"This *hope* we** have as an anchor of the soul, both sure and steadfast, and which enters the Presence ***behind*** the veil." So we see that the Holy Spirit himself has told us that we can have confidence in His promises because of the **"immutability"** of His promise to Abraham.

And Romans 9-11 discusses this absolute reliability of the promises that God made so long ago to the ancient nation of Israel. For Romans 9 begins with the words:

> "I tell the truth in Christ, I am not lying, my conscience also bearing me witness in the Holy Spirit, that I have great sorrow and continual grief in my heart. For I could wish that I myself were accursed from Christ for my brethren, my countrymen according to the flesh, who are Israelites, to whom *pertain* the adoption, the glory, the covenants, the giving of the law, the service *of God,* and the promises; of whom *are* the fathers and from whom, according to the flesh, Christ *came,* who is over all, *the* eternally blessed God. Amen." (Romans 9:1-5)

Here, we need to notice that one of the things it says **"*pertain*"** to Paul's **"brethren,"** his **"countrymen according to the flesh, who are Israelites,"** is **"the promises."**

And in Romans 11, the main part of the three chapter argument ends with the words:

> "For I do not desire, brethren, that you should be ignorant of this mystery, lest you should be wise in your own opinion, that blindness in part has happened to Israel until the fullness of the Gentiles has come in. And so all Israel will be saved, as it is written: 'The Deliverer will come out of Zion, And He will turn away ungodliness from Jacob; For this is My covenant with them, When I take away their sins.' Concerning the gospel *they are* enemies for your sake, but concerning the election *they are* beloved for the sake of the fathers. For the gifts and the calling of God *are* irrevocable." (Romans 11:25-29)

So we see that the absolute reliability of these promises made to the ancient nation of Israel is indeed fundamental to the Christian faith, even though many godly Christians do not realize it.

Conclusion

How very much should the truths in this book affect the hearts and minds of the people of God! And how they would affect our lives, if we were to truly follow everything our Lord taught us. For **"if we walk in the light as He is in the light, we have fellowship with one another, and the blood of Jesus Christ His Son cleanses us from all sin."** (1 John 1:7) But we all fail so often. **"For we all stumble in many things."** (James 3:2) But **"if anyone sins, we have an Advocate with the Father, Jesus Christ the righteous."** (1 John 2:1) And **"If we confess our sins, He is faithful and just to forgive us *our* sins and to cleanse us from all unrighteousness."** (1 John 1:9) So we need to keep short accounts with God, confessing our sins as soon as we realize we have committed them. And to remember our Lord's promises that **"Blessed *are* those who hunger and thirst for righteousness, For they shall be filled."** (Matthew 5:6) And **"He who testifies to these things says, 'Surely I am coming quickly.'"** To which our hearts respond, **"Amen. Even so, come, Lord Jesus!"** (Revelation 22:20)

This little book is sent out with a prayer that it would be a blessing to the people of God, those for whom our beloved Lord, Jesus the Christ, suffered at Calvary. He purchased us with His own blood, and He loves us beyond measure.

James C. Morris
December, 2022